MW00861705

BREAKING
THE
GODSPELL

ABOUT THE AUTHOR

Neil Freer is a futant researcher, writer, lecturer, and creator of philosophical "models" living on the Pacific Rim. His undergraduate work was in English and graduate work in Philosophy. He has taught Philosophy and History of Religion ("back in the days of transition") and given private seminars. He is an avowed generalist, a proponent of dyadic fusion (sexual partners moving consciously up the metamorphic evolutionary ladder together) and is one of the five or six persons on the planet most optimistic about the future of the human race. He has also been instrumental in developing software for industry and personal use.

DEDICATION

To the Human Race, genetically created, deprived of immortality,now realizing our beginnings and glory, emerging from our planetary adolescence. To the Nefilim our creators, half-parents and sometimes cruel masters, perhaps curious watchers of our progress.
May we both evolve and transcend.

BREAKING THE GODSPELL

The Politics of Our Evolution

By
Neil Freer

Introduced by
Zecharia Sitchin

Published 2000
The Book Tree
Escondido, CA

Breaking the Godspell:
The Politics of Our Evolution
ISBN 978-1-58509-560-5

First Edition: 1987
Second Printing: 1990
Third Printing (revised edition): 1994
Fourth Printing: 2000

Cover design: Darlene Olivia McElroy

Cover depiction: The god, Sharruma, gives instructions and directions to his foreman (king) Tudhaliya. Hittite rock relief at Yasilikaya (central modern Turkey), about 1250 B.C.

Contact the author via email at freer1@concentric.net

Published by
The Book Tree
Post Office Box 724
Escondido, CA 92033

We provide fascinating and educational products to help awaken the public to new ideas and information that would not be available otherwise. Call **(800) 700-TREE** for our *FREE BOOK TREE CATALOG* or visit our website at www.thebooktree.com for more information.

ACNOWLEDGEMENTS

The author is pleased to acknowledge the following for their kindness in permitting the use of quotations. Zecharia Sitchin and his publishers Stein and Day for use of material from the original printing of *The Twelfth Planet*, the first book of The Earth Chronicle Series (New York, Stein and Day, 1976). *The Stairway to Heaven*, (New York, Avon, 1980): *The Wars of Gods and Men*, (New York, Avon, 1985) and a fourth book not yet published are highly recommended though not quoted. Timothy Leary and New Falcon Publications, Phoenix, Arizona for quotes from *The Game of Life* (1993) and *Info-Psychology*, (1987). Stan Tenen of the Meru Foundation (P.O. Box 1738, San Anselmo, CA 94960) for references to material in issues of their bulletin, *Torus*. Stan has insisted that I emphasize that the work is "speculative, in the preliminary stages, and in great need of copious academic polishing." I do so with a great deal of respect for his meticulously high standards. Quotation from the work of T.B. Pawlicki with the permission of Prentice Hall Publishing Co. from *How to Build A Flying Saucer: And Other Proposals In Speculative Engineering* (Englewood Cliffs, NJ: Prentice Hall, 1981). Quotes from the work of C.W. Ceram published with the permission of Alfred A. Knopf from *Gods, Graves and Scholars* translated by Edward B. Garside and Sophie Wilkins copyright 1967. Quotes from the work of E. A. Speiser by permission of Yale University Press from *Ancient Mesopotamia*, (pages 35-76 in Dentan, R.C. (editor), *The Idea of History in the Ancient Near East* American Oriental Series 38, (New Haven: Yale University Press and Oxford University Press, London, 1855), pp. 49-50. General references to the work *of* Stephen Jay Gould with the permission *of W. W.* Norton Co. from *Ever Since Darwin* (New York, W.W. Norton, 1977). Quote from the work of Rene Noorbergen reprinted with permission of MacMillan Publishing Co. from *Secrets of the Lost Races* by Rene Noorbergen, copyright 1977 by Rene Noorbergen. The article by David Pilbeam, Ph.D, "The Descent of Hominoids and Hominids", March 1984 is reprinted by permission of Scientific American through Freeman. The quote from Edward O. Wilson's, *Sociobiology*, abridged edition, by permission of Harvard University Press, Cambridge, MA copyright 1980. Excerpt from an interview with Edward De Bano, in OMNI, March 1985 copyright 1985 by Anthony Liversidge reprinted with the permission of OMNI Publications International Limited. Quote from *The Aquarian Conspiracy*, (Los Angeles, Tarcher, 1980) with permission from Marilyn Ferguson through Pat Perrin, copyright 1980 by Marilyn Ferguson. Quote from Merlin Stone's, *When God Was A Woman*, (San Diego, New York, London, Harcourt Brace Jovanovich, A Harvest/HBJ Book, 1976) by permission of Doubleday Publishers, copyright 1976. Quote from John Naisbitt's *Megatrends* by permission of Warner Books, New York, copyright 1982, 1984 by John Naisbitt.

TABLE OF CONTENTS

INTRODUCTION
BY ZECHARIA SITCHIN

Who are we?
Why are we here? Where did we come from?
Are we unique?
How did it all begin?

It is now more than a decade since I had posed those questions in my book *The 12th Planet*—rhetorical questions, to be sure, setting the stage for articulating my answers: and yet not questions cleverly posed as the opening for a book, but questions that had troubled me and weighed on my mind since childhood.

I have been asked often how did I embark on the long search (a lifetime!) that culminated with *The Earth Chronicles* series of books. The answer I give is worth repeating here. It was at school in Tel-Aviv; we reached in our Bible studies Chapter VI of Genesis—the story of the Great Flood or Deluge. It begins with several enigmatic verses, undoubtedly the remnant of a longer text, that describe the circumstances on Earth just prior to the Deluge. They tell us—in the familiar King James translation—that "when men began to multiply on the face of the earth, and daughters were born unto them, that the sons of God saw the daughters of men that they were fair; and they took them wives of all which they chose... There were giants in the earth in those days, and also after that, when the sons of God came in unto the daughters of men and they bare children to them, the same became mighty men who were of old, men of renown."

Fortunately we were studying the Old Testament in its original Hebrew language; and the word that is commonly translated *giants* is, in the Hebrew text, NEFILIM. So young Sitchin raised his hand and asked, "Excuse me my teacher, but why do you say 'giants' when the word Nefilim means, "Those Who Had Come Down?" Whereupon the teacher said, "Sit down, Sitchin, you don't question the Bible."

But I had not questioned the Bible—I had questioned an interpretation of a biblical verse. That question, unanswered at that time, is the starting point of my quest. Why did the Bible, so precise in its original language, call the "sons of God" (what a statement in a Jewish Bible!)

iii

iv   *Breaking the God-Spell*

"Those Who Had Come Down"?—obviously from the heights of heaven to the face of the Earth.

In accepting my interpretation and identification of the *Nefilim* and making this point a foundation stone of his current book *Breaking The God-Spell*, Neil Freer has indeed put his finger not only on the outcome of my researches, but also on their very root and beginning.

It was 1876 when the scholarly and religious worlds were shaken by the publication of George Smith's *The Chaldean Account of Genesis*, followed by L.S. King's *The Seven Tablets of Creation*. Since then scholars and theologians alike have come to recognize that the Creation tales of the Bible are condensed and edited versions of texts that were first written on clay tablets in Sumer, where Man's first known (post-Diluvial) civilization began some 6,000 years ago.

A century later, in *The 12th Planet* (1976) I have shown that those texts were no primitive myths, but depositories of advanced scientific knowledge with which modern scholars are only now beginning to catch up.

It is gratifying that a mere decade after publication of my work, an author with the grasp that Neil Freer displays in *Breaking The God-Spell* has set out to probe what the recognition of the existence and Earth-visits of the Nefilim can mean not just to scientists and theologians, but to each human being upon this planet Earth.

Zecharia Sitchin
New York, March 1987

CHAPTER 1
OVERVIEW

A retrospective examination of our brief history on this planet makes it rather clear that periodically certain overviews are attained of that melodrama that afford us the opportunity as a race to understand ourselves better and to control our individual and racial destiny with a greater measure of intelligence. That may be called reaching a new level of consciousness or a new plateau of development.

From a certain perspective it is clear that the pressures of crisis seem to be the most common stimuli for both technological and philosophic change. It is important to recognize, however, that there must be some raw material, both technological and/or philosophical, with which to fashion the new implements or concepts. The raw material for technological change comes through scientific research and development catalyzed by generous amounts of intuition. New philosophical paradigms come from the comprehensive vision of the creative generalist. Although it is easiest to write the social equation in the linear form of crisis pressure causing reactant change the complexity of the real situation is obviously much more circular.

From a negative point of view, our current planetary situation is one of classic crisis. Whether it be the recognition that, on some nondescript afternoon, we could commit nuclear racial suicide without really wanting to, or we have created planetary ecological disasters, or betray our common heritage and permit other humans to starve or whatever, it is generally agreed that we are "at the brink" of a "racial crisis" that has brought us to a "turning point" in our history. Reactions vary from the debilitating fear that some deranged person will push the button that triggers our annihilation to the optimistic view that "doomsday has been cancelled" due to the fact that we must cooperate to explore the "new frontier" of space with its relatively unlimited resources, relieving the pressures of competitive survival. We are experiencing a "vision gap" in the view of Barbara Marx Hubbard. Timothy Leary has characterized the syndrome as "navigational" in the sense that we have "lost the map . . . misplaced the genetic code." But, by all of these acknowledgements, our collective consciousness recognizes that it's time both to radically alter the status quo on the planet and to leave the planet and make the trek to the stars; there is no question in my mind that is a far more powerful force than the negative effect of the possibility of self-annihilation.

This planet is on hold . . .

But, if one understands what is really happening, the picture is one of exhilarating expectation and promise. In the greatest perspective, setting aside the short-sighted bickering and barbaric violence of the senile establishments as only a decadent residue perpetuated by a vanishing element within the species, the grand picture of the activity of the race today is very exciting.

Like a single-cell organism about to go through asexual reproduction by binary-fission so the race is about to produce another version of itself, a new species, this time adapted to space and space-time travel. Biological analogies are very appropriate. Like the individual cell members of the colony mold that, under the stimulus of certain ambient conditions, secretes a specific catalytic chemical, gathers together and forms a plant-like stalk which buds at the top and gives off cells to be carried to other places where the conditions are possibly better, so we, under the stimulus of the crowding, pollution, radiation, boredom, and our genetic programming, haltingly push upward on the glowing shaft of the rocket and will soon be disseminating spore to the planets and the distant star systems.

Yet one thing is extremely clear: this planet is on hold.

It is easy to perceive that all of our major social, political, economic, philosophical and religious systems have evolved individually and interactively to a natural point where they no longer serve the purpose for which they were instituted, no longer are relevant to the needs of the time, no longer reflect the collective thinking and orientation which conceived and accepted them, no longer support the efforts they were designed to facilitate, no longer even exhibit the characteristics of their intended form. And we should certainly not be surprised. If we experience constant change in ourselves individually and collectively so should we expect the same developmental patterns in the institutions we have engendered.

We are producing technological change at an amazing rate. But technological change, although certainly important, is not what is essential at this point; it is simply an advanced stage of the ongoing Industrial Revolution which has been with us for some time.

But, at the same time, there are strong currents of thought and feeling throughout the world that we all must come together, that our vision is expanding, that there is an almost unthinkable possibility of cooperation that will transcend the black barbarism of war, that the sparks of conscious, intelligent unity will become a symbolic flame. The current of thought in

When it's paradigm time it paradigms . . .

almost every area of human existence and in every discipline is moving toward a new unifying concept. All signs are pointing to a central, integrating paradigm that will complete and fulfill the meaning of each. It is clear that we, as a race, are about to experience the most radical, global, all-encompassing revolution in our history. That revolution will be in the way we perceive and understand ourselves most fundamentally. But, although the signs all point in the same direction, until now the destination has been obscured.

A paradigm is defined as "an outstandingly clear pattern, example or archetype." The ideas contained in the new paradigm presented herein are not for the weak. Yet there is no way of presenting them without their profound implications being immediately felt, regardless of how skillfully they are presented and how much attention is given to the dictum derived from Kuhn's work on scientific revolutions, viz. that new ideas are best presented as extensions of a previous paradigm rather than exhibiting the characteristics of catastrophe theory events. It is all too true that, when the newness of an idea is just extreme enough, we often reflexively recoil as if our minds had no real primary control over our reactions. The threshold obviously is reached when the idea is sufficiently powerful to threaten to remove the framework of the paradigm of reality with which our minds have been working. Humor is the key to any difficult transition.

It was my conviction for some time that the vectors of thought and exploration expressing the leading edge of our rapid development as a species had finally brought us to a point where we understood ourselves sufficiently to transcend the primitive elements in our traditions which caused such terrible divisions between us. I thought, then, in the prevalent terms of a linear and continuous general and racial evolutionary process paralleled by the recapitulative ontogenetic development of the individual. I had to live with the fact that the paleontologists seemed to be scrapping a major theory a month, our ancient history seemed to be riddled with contradictions, that we did not seem to really know who and what we were, all justified on the basis that more research and exploration needed to be done. But there were disturbing elements that would not be put away: the religious doctrines and organizations and beliefs whose persistence in existence could not wholly be explained by the attraction to comfortable consensual reality-tunnels or even "robot" imprinting; the tenacity of the

Every word of this book is meant to cause a revolution, a gentle revolution in the way we conceive of ourselves individually and as a planetary race.

ancient legends and "myths" to which obviously intelligent and sophisticated humans had assigned such a high and serious importance for such a long time; ultimately the gnawing puzzlement bordering on suspicion caused by the vehemence with which the ancient "gods" and their worship was assailed by the churches. Nothing persists in the worldwide common consciousness for thousands of years, enduring suppression, ridicule, and contempt without having some element of truth to sustain it. If "gods" were not so related to the Judaeo-Christian "God" and the concept of worship was still understood in its original meaning of "work for", things might have been easier. When I came to examining the evidence from archeology I realized that the last key pieces of the mystery of our past were available to us.

Every word of this book is meant to cause a revolution, a gentle revolution in the way we conceive of ourselves individually and as a planetary race. To achieve that purpose I examine and interpret the content and direction of our major disciplines and currents of thought, demonstrating how they all are inexorably pointing toward a new synthesis, then draw the framework of that new paradigm to explain the puzzle of human existence. To those who have not previously considered it a puzzle, I suggest that a situation that generates questions as fundamental as where did we come from, what is our purpose here if any, where are we going etc. fits the category quite well. This book deals with the last pieces of that puzzle as they fall, rather quietly, into place without our much realizing it, and the reasons why we don't much realize it, and what the picture really looks like once those last pieces are in place. When it's paradigm time it paradigms.

Because of the attraction of novelty we tend to look forward rather than backward. Yet, as we explore the future, the explorers of the past—the archeologists, the archeoastronomers, the experts in ancient languages, the historians and the paleontologists—have gradually accumulated a vast store of information about our past, our origins. As we look backwards now we see a brightness, a glow of knowledge and an expanding worldwide pattern that is as exciting as the future. Every discipline and facet of our lives are pregnant with anticipatory signs but the catalytic element is found in the area of history and prehistory. Although the new paradigm has its source in the human psyche the key to its realization is found in a seemingly quiet science—archeology—where the last key pieces of the puzzle have finally been derived. Developments in the area of archeology have gone relatively

Information in this area has evolved to a whole new dimension . . .

unnoticed, and yet the implications may be of even greater shock value than many other scientific findings in the long term. The methodical work of archeologists in the Middle East has unearthed, restored, cataloged and evaluated well over five hundred thousand artifacts and documents, located the sites of biblical and pre-biblical history, unearthed whole towns, palaces, and cities. Documents, contracts, instructional texts, astronomical catalogs, even detailed histories and chronologies have been translated.

The overview provided by the synthesis of the information that has been amassed from the work of many disciplines points to two general facts: the accounts in the Old Testament, although condensed from more detailed accounts pre-dating them, are true and accurate in their most minute detail and the evidence supports the fact that the "god" or "gods" of the Old Testament and the New were not and is not some transcendent infinite Being but an advanced race of humanoids, the Nefilim mentioned in Genesis, who created man, as we know ourselves, for their own practical purposes.

It should be emphasized that this is not a discovery but a *re-discovery*. The ancient authors of the documents recovered from the archeological digs recorded the facts accurately; any misunderstanding or misinterpretation or distortion has been the result of the action of subsequent generations over time.

Most of us are well aware that opinions and theories of this nature have been extant for quite some time. In the recent past we have been able to view the television documentation of the sites and wonders of the ancient world that have moved Von Dainiken and others to speculate along these lines with a great deal of conviction. It is to be noted, however, that the scholarship and information in this area has evolved to a whole new dimension through the work of a long progession of scholars and researchers culminating in the recent work of Zecharia Sitchin. Through their efforts and Sitchin's master synthesis we have at hand the information we need to define our origin as an historical event in its true nature as well as the scientific knowledge to comprehend and verify that what we are examining is possible. The rejection of the flat earth theory or the geocentric theory of the universe, or the most profound discovery of science pales in the light of this realization. The simple fact of the matter is that there is no facet, no detail of human existence as we know it that is not effected by the

The last piece of the puzzle of the human condition has fallen into place . . .

revelation of the nature of our real beginning. As with most new ideas, we have gone through several phases of discovery and reactive attitudes. The early signs of questioning are well exemplified in the writings of Von Dainiken who brought to popular awareness the enigmatic artifacts and strange sites around the world that were the basis for his conjectures about the possibility of "extraterrestrial visitors," "astronaut gods" and UFOs. The second stage is personified by the various scientists, especially in NASA, such as Maurice Chatelain, former head of the Apollo communications division, who began to recognize the possibility of a technological explanation for some of the more mystifying and even bizarre events recounted in the Old Testament of the Bible. The third general stage has come through the work of Sitchin who fulfills and synthesizes the accurate parts of both the mainstream and the dissenting points of view regarding the real nature of the "gods" and our true origins.

The ramifications of such knowledge produces an immediate illumination of both the present and the future. Our institutions, social forms, political modes, customs, traditions, philosophy, religion, are all, when reexamined, shown to be influenced profoundly by our concept of ourselves as a result of that redifinition. The essence of the synthesis put forth is that, almost without notice, the last piece of the puzzle of the human condition has fallen into place and the revelation is the impetus for the unfolding of the next stage of the maturation of the race. And what an excitingly magnificent potential we have for that transition.

Consider the advances we have made in that direction. The ability to do genetic engineering enables us, literally, to create a new human race. The possibility of longevity and relative immortality is real and immanent. Travel to the stars is (questionable pun) only a matter of space-time and interplanetary travel taken for granted. Quantum physics has provided the real possibility of a grand unified field theory and what has been described as "the language of the universe"—as well as the most adequate vocabulary to describe the most evolved human psychology. The intelligent use of psychopharmaceuticals has furnished us the keys to the doors of perception through which we may pass to explore the interior universe at will. The rapid development of computers may well bring the advent of aspects of an artifical intelligence superior in some respects to the human that created it. The communication of information, which has been growing exponentially,

This work is a primer of transition to generic humanity.

has become extremely fast impressing the fact of the unity of the global village. The national budgets of the major nations of the world allocate taxpayers' money to build space colonies. We are ready.

It is my objective to create a catalytic situation in which the increasing glow of knowledge from the past, fusing with the brightness of the future, can illuminate the present. Will we forever continue to talk to each other like children afraid to uncover their eyes in the fear of seeing an imagined ghost? Will we say that it is not possible that we can progress beyond our past, that everything has been learned, that the fears of some of our ancestors must be the burdensome fears of our children and keep us separated forever?

Unshackled from the cramping concept of a God who can act as peevishly and cruelly as the Nefilim individuals literally did at times, we are free to seek to understand the ultimate nature of the universe and whatever level of comprehension we may attain of possible universes, and to seek to understand and put ourselves in harmony with whatever ultimate Principle we can fathom.

We have at hand the information we need to achieve the overview under which every separate discipline, every institution, every mode of our existence comes together in a picture that is both familiar and yet amazingly new.

The unification of the race, once the barriers based on the piously misconstrued interpretations of doctrines influencing politics, economics, science, philosophy and world views gradually fall away, is now a realizable ideal.

This work is a primer of transition to generic humanity. It is not polemical. It is not an apologetic for the evidence for the true nature of our origins. Rather, it simply takes the fact of our being created by an advanced race, the Nefilim spoken of in Genesis, as verified and uses it as the catalytic key point which can unify the myriad indicative trends toward a new planetary consciousness and unlock the racial, planetary blocks we experience. It is preoccupied with the fascinating, exciting possiblities opened thereby for the present and the future. It suggests the knowledge opened to us for scientific advancement, the significance of the information now available to us for the acceleration of our racial maturation. It advances a new design of human nature and existence with a view to the next stage, a quantum jump in human and racial consciousness.

Is there any more vitally exciting, challenging, constructive enterprise in which to immerse ourselves and initiate our children?

It is obvious that a view of human nature as a genetically engineered creation has risk involved with it. The problem of criteria is involved directly here. Our time is oriented to the scientific method as a criterion of certainly. The techniques of archeology can be methodical, scrupulously meticulous, performed by persons of the highest integrity, ethical standards and mature judgement. But there is no way that rigorously controlled, repeatable experiments can be used here; in a court of law the evidence would be called circumstantial. It is not a matter of simply accepting a curious, previously unknown scientific bit of information that is only of incidental effect. It profoundly affects every aspect of human existence. I am well aware that there is always the possibility of misinterpretation, wishful projection or premature conclusions. I can only say simply that, in view of the direct evidence from the recovered records reinforced by the questions which are unanswerable unless the evidence is accepted, I am as firmly convinced that we have arrived at the correct solution as I am aware of the risk.

In view of the known pace at which we collectively accommodate to major change, it may take generations to assimilate and restructure—but is there any more vitally exciting, challenging, constructive enterprise in which to immerse ourselves and initiate our children?

CHAPTER 2

A THOUGHT EXPERIMENT

The beliefs a person holds determine what he will perceive of reality.
According to Magellan's log book, cited by Lawrence Blair in Rhythms of
Vision, the barefoot natives of Patagonia could not see the European ships
when they arrived at South America for the first time. To the aborigines,
the shore party appeared out of thin air on the beach. Eventually the
shamans discerned a faint image of the tall ships riding anchor offshore.
They pointed the images out to their tribespeople, and after everyone
concentrated on the concept of giant sailing ships for a long time, the
galleons materialized. And then the aborigines were annihilated by cultural
shock.[1]

T.B. Pawlicki

Imagine yourself as a member of a planetary civilization that has
developed sufficiently to begin to systematically reexamine (RE-search) its
past and reevaluate its myths, legends and history. It has reached a point in
its technological development where its science fiction will be tomorrow's
reality.

Suddenly the feats of the heroes of the planet's past, their flights through
space and the atmosphere, their incredible technology, their loves and wars,
the enigmatic events of the sacred histories and "myths" involving ancient
divine beings, the creation stories, viewed in the light of what is now known
to be technologically possible, are not only verified by the archeological and
scientific evidence as literally true, but show that the primitive religious
beliefs about the ancient gods are the result of the fact that those ancient
gods, now understood as of the same general genetic type as the race,
created your race by genetic engineering, a process only recently discovered
by your race's scientists.

As an intelligent member of your race, you suddenly are confronted with
the ramifications of that knowledge. You see that the entire structure of the
civilization and culture in which you have lived and been conditioned must
now be fundamentally reevaluated. You see clearly that the political
framework of your society, basing itself in general on the traditional
religious beliefs and ethical systems, must be reconstructed to mirror the
new realization of the true nature and freedom of a human individual.

Those who can adjust to the new vision of humankind . . . will welcome the new dimension of human dignity as we emerge from the cocoon of ignorance and servitude.

Political and religious debates seem as arguments between stone age tribal leaders over cargo cult traditions and you realize that there is already begun, on the part of the more intelligent and ruthless of the sectarian elements and their leaders, a rapid re-posturing and proclamation of their exclusive position as representatives of the Makers—whose true nature, they say, they always knew but held as secret doctrine because the masses were not ready for it. Governments, religions, scholars, "experts," the vested interests, react as profoundly threatened, secretly feel like fools, struggle frantically to keep their status and power. They suppress information, attempt to control education, claim insufficient proof and warping of the facts in the teeth of conclusive evidence while they themselves manipulate, censor, and even punish their members in a contradiction of their principles justifying all on the basis of claiming to protect their members and the world against the "false doctrines."

If it sounds at once like science fiction yet uncomfortably familiar, your reaction is correct. The place is planet Earth; the scenario is slightly ahead of time by only a few short years. This shock from the past will effect those who react negatively as deeply as Alvin Toffler's personal fears of the future shocked him.

Those who can adjust to the new vision of humankind and the awesome possibilities it opens up, can expand into the freedom and responsibilities it allows, can put energy into the creation of a new planetary future, will welcome the new dimension of human dignity as we emerge from the cocoon of ignorance and servitude.

The turning point in world-wide public awareness has already been foreshadowed in the content of the televised "Heritage" program presented in conjunction with the celebration of the Jewish New Year on October 1, 1984. Abba Eban, the narrator, drew an unequivocal distinction between the legal agreement entered into by the progenitors of the tribe of Juddah with "one of the gods" they recognized as a local personage and the later "vision" of that god being universal developed under David, appointed as go-between by that god. The original contract gave the tribe the patronage and protection they needed in exchange for their observing the laws laid down by their god. The "vision" of that god's authority, expanded to "universal" status gave their aggressive expansion into neighboring territory, on order of that god, the character of a crusade—with his emblem on their war banners.

Then, with the explosive reaction of world religions, embarrassed scholars, miffed experts, the firestorm hits.

A very plausible extension of the scenario would project the turning point, the critical event bringing the facts to world-wide attention, as a well-timed, authoritative, grave statement by the government of Israel or perhaps the Israel Exploration Society acting with its approval, detailing concisely the conclusive evidence gathered from the intensive, systematic archeological digs, scientific and linguistic analysis and scholarly interpretation being carried on even now under the watchful Uzis. The potential rending of the Jewish fabric, the orthodox against the liberal, would already have been addressed, perhaps negotiated, if not resolved, before the official statement.

The clear definition of the humanoid nature of the gods, the recognition of the real roots of the Hebrew religion, coupled with the recognition of the earlier creation of humans by the Nefilim in Sumer would seem to be an all but self-destructive act on the part of the Jews. But the carefully orchestrated, powerful message, presented in a scientific documentary format, establishes the image of Israel as an erudite, enlightened, progressive nation setting the standard for the rest of the world by calmly and confidently transcending a past now seen as relatively primitive in modern perspective.

The honest appraisal steals the fire from Moslem, Christian, Hindu, et.al. Israel becomes the world's instructor in things archeological and historical; the Israeli archeologists carry off one of the most satisfying coups in scientific history; astute insinuations set the stage for an unprecedented transcendence of cultural-religious-political conflicts in the Middle East; young intellectual Jews dance ecstatically in the streets and on campuses; for a brief moment Israel has all the character of the world's graduate school. Then, with the explosive reaction of world religions, conservative politicians, embarrassed scholars, miffed experts, disconcerted teachers, the firestorm hits.

Again, if it sounds far-fetched but uncomfortably possible, you are correct. In fact, a member of the Israel Exploration Society, Zecharia Sitchin, has already written three books of detailed analysis that, *working from nothing but the archaeological evidence now at hand,* present a solid and scholarly case based on thirty years of research.

Interestingly, and probably understandably in the context of modern society, the reaction of many not associated with religion is often "so what?"

**Trend analysis will tend to miss the subject almost completely
at this point in time.**

---

or how come it is not in the news?" or, on the part of the better read, "why
do I not see this in the trend analysis literature?"

The simple answer to the simple "so what?" is that the Western culture in
which we live is grounded in the Judaeo-Christian tradition which now is
seen in a totally different light. Every facet of our life and those around us is
touched by this fact even though an individual may not ascribe to any of
those doctrines explicitly. Closer examination of our philosophical, psychological, sociological, political and ethical views show them to be impregnated
with traditions and perspectives that we never thought were not our own.
"The beliefs a person holds determine the way he sees reality."

It is fascinating how we manage to consign this type of view so
consistently to the category of the "interesting"—which thereby allows us
to examine and play with it but not do anything about it. If it is relegated to
the category of the mysterious or the sensational like UFOs or Bigfoot it
becomes titillating but manageable—so it tends to show up in those
publications dealing in the sensational and having a less than solid
reputation for solid journalism. For an establishment newspaper or
magazine, economically sensitive to powerful organizations, to seriously
espouse the subject would be surprising at this point. It may be a matter of
interest to the individual but it is of grave import to organized religion.

Trend analysis will tend to miss the subject almost completely at this
point in time. It is currently the fashion of analysts to eschew the title of
futurist, to structure their image as no-nonsense, hard-fact, sincere,
benevolent persons who rely on vast computer data bases for their material.
We certainly can profit by their genuine and valuable contributions. But
trend analysis extrapolates from the now, the statistically assigned
importance of facts usually being determined by what gets through the
news window in the press or by some version of interpretation by econo-
political impact. If you have enough data about the performance of the tree
you can say, rather comfortably, what the next few feet of trunk will look
like.

And, ultimately, who will teach the facts? Teachers in our school systems
who are afraid of their jobs if they teach evolutionary theory or even
encourage their students to form their own opinions? College professors
whose careers have been based on the traditional history-or-myth approach?
Religious leaders whose entire context is a militant denial of the information?

The position of the honest archeologist becomes increasingly uncomfortable . . .

Occultists who have developed complicated "spiritual" explanations?

Simply stated, this development is the critical variable ignored or missed in the "megatrends" projected by Naisbitt, the shrewd extrapolations of Cetron, the scenarios of Kahn, the conspiracies of Ferguson, the ecological theology of Capra, and the techno-vision of O'Neill, Berry, Gilfillan, Dyson.

Intensive archeological work in the Mideast, Egypt, and the Indus Valley has produced huge quantities of artifacts and, even more importantly, such a tremendous number of documents that some of them have not even been translated yet. The position of the honest archeologist becomes increasingly uncomfortable in that the traditional interpretation of any reference to the "gods" as "myth" becomes more and more untenable. One can only be amused by the bitter resentment exhibited by a scholar who, on reading the actual accounts contained in recovered documents of the life and deeds of one of the gods, Ishtar (Inanna, Astarte, Anat, Anthat, Athena: an aviatrix, politically powerful among her peers, famed as manipulative and sexually promiscuous, a skilled warrior) complained bitterly that the facts did not befit someone who was of "mythological" stature! It would have been a bit easier to accept if her humanoid status had been recognized for what it was.

The evidence has been at hand for some time, waiting only for our technological development to show us that indeed it could be so, needing only the keys for interpretation. The game has changed; the truth is beyond our expectations, the ramifications are inescapable. If we keep our sense of humor, we may evolve to racial adulthood rather gracefully.

CHAPTER 3
THE "GODS"
AND VERY GRAVE SCHOLARS

The mind has lost its cutting edge, we hardly understand the Ancients.
                                        Gregoire de Tours, 6th century A.D.

For we need to understand the past five thousand years in order to master
the next hundred years.
                        Gods, Graves, and Scholars, C.W. Ceram[2]

An understanding of the development of our concept of history—*it has not always been as we are familiar with it now*—reveals a great deal about the way our thinking about the ancient past and our beginnings has been formed. We need to step back collectively from our history in order to gain insight concerning the psychology of our perception of the past. An essential facet of the new planetary paradigm is an accurate, global, unitary view of the history of the human race as free as possible of national, cultural, academic or religious bias not just for the purpose of avoiding conflict, but because that is the essential nature of our situation in the first place.

History, in the accepted western academic meaning, is *written* tradition. Prehistory, although having the overtones, through popular usage, of "very ancient" and "primitive," is really a quite relative term. With reference to any culture, it means the time when that culture had no written records. In that context many of the cultures of the world were "prehistoric" down to the beginning of the nineteenth century. The concept "prehistoric" in itself is only five generations old at most. We are only able to even think in those terms because of the relatively recent perspective afforded by the data accumulated from the findings of the geologist and the biologist. Using stratigraphic techniques coupled with the even more recent carbon and other types of dating, their findings support the work of the prehistorian, the archeologist dealing with the area of prehistory.

We tend to look on the records of our history as some immutable set of facts. We should correct that view to see the records of our past as a collection of subjective impressions, most often written considerably after the event, which has had many writers and many editors. It is the editors who have chosen to leave out or delete some material, who have exercised

It is difficult to avoid the cultural lens effect.

sincere but erroneous judgement in some cases, who have been biased by cultural, nationalistic or peer pressures who have caused more problems than original authors. We owe both a great debt for their efforts—but the best of them would be the first to caution us that we need to keep their work in proper perspective.

The words "god" and "divine," so freely used by modern scholars when referring to the personages revered by the ancients were not used by the Sumerians or the Akkadians who referred to those beings as "lord" and did not consider them divine in the sense that we understand that word. The word "heaven" means one thing for the Western mind and a totally different thing for the ancient Sumerians. The use of these terms without constant redifinition is a compromise for the sake of convention. Even the definitions of history and prehistory that were stated above are substantially conventions of western cultural orientation. It is difficult to avoid the cultural lens effect. As a Westerner and an American it is one thing to understand the facts and characteristics of the six thousand year old traditions of the Chinese or the Indian civilizations but it is radically another to feel and think as an individual of another culture reading the same records.

To concern oneself with the character and history of Western historical writing and interpretation from the earliest times—and there have been books written entirely on that subject—is to immediately encounter a striking and significant fact. The craft of the historian exhibits a well defined pattern of evolution through a number of phases, each identified by forced changes in perspective, attitude and method, a not unexpected characteristic in the light of improved information handling and scientific advancement. But, whereas one might think, at first, that, for the Western mind, the development of a comprehensive and coherent history of our habitation of this planet would resemble an almost nostalgic, systematic rummaging through the attics of our mostly known past to verify, clarify and organize details, one soon realizes that the process, in its negative aspect, actually more closely resembles the gradual recovery of a person from self-induced amnesia. If a single word had to be used to characterize the cause of that cultural amnesia it most accurately would be *denial* and the sharply defined focal point of that denial is the period of our very beginning. But focusing on the negative threads in the rich fabric of our rapid cultural development would lead inevitably to assignment of blame and inane polemics of which

Western written history shows a definite pattern of continual sophistication and maturation while going through radical changes of interpretive premises.

there is already too much in the literature. In the largest overview of our history we can clearly discern the unmistakable process of psychological maturation and that process precludes any assignment of blame greater in degree than that applying to the sincere mistakes of the adolescent working at social maturity. Since the historian is a part of that process it is not surprising that Western written history shows a definite pattern of continual sophistication and maturation while at the same time going through various stages of radical change of interpretive premises. As a result, the history of Western culture's historiography (that body of information which has been interpreted and written by those authorities who mold the academic textbooks and influence the opinions of other experts) may be summarized by describing how the historians have *interpreted* their material in any given age. Historiography in the West has passed through three major phases and is now entering a fourth. Since the Christian era in Europe and America is a central and dominant influence we may understand these phases as the pre-Christian, the Christian, the post-Christian, and resolution phases. These divisions are generalized and only excusable as means of simplifying the explanation.

To survey the changes in attitude toward history and its interpretation in Western culture we must start at the beginnings of historiography as manifest in the work of the Sumerian archivists. We have the writing of the Greeks and the Romans, closer to us by two to three thousand years, only in a few handfuls of fragments of documents predominantly through second and third hand sources. By comparison, we have the Sumerians and their successors in one half *million* documents on clay tablets, many not even translated yet because of the sheer volume. Roughly eighty percent of that documentation consists of records of legal matters, contracts, inventories, lexicons and texts on many subjects and twenty percent is made up of historical and official literature. We can paint a far better picture of the details of the daily lives of the Sumerians than we can of the Romans. We do not have to depend on the excavation of an isolated disaster such as Pompeii; we have the 25,000 odd pieces of the seventh century B.C. bi-lingual library collected by Assurbanipal at Nineveh. Although the Sumerian era had been all but lost to the Western world for centuries, it was recognized as the "cradle of civilization" soon after its rediscovery in the late 1800s when interest was once again shown in the ancient past, first through a faddish and fashionable collecting spree and then by a few pioneer amateur

What was gradually uncovered and deciphered proved to be mind-boggling in its sophistication, immensity and grandeur.

---

archeologists who actually began digging in ruins guided by descriptions and clues in the fragments of ancient literature. The successes were immediate, interpretations many times doubtful, the languages mysterious and the work hard and too often a treasure hunt rather than a methodical quest. But the success of the driven amateur could not be ignored for long and soon professional scholars became involved and methodical techniques of meticulous digging, identification by strata, and preservation were developed. What was gradually uncovered and deciphered proved to be mind-boggling in its sophistication, immensity and grandeur. The complex picture of huge cities of great wealth, teeming with commercial enterprise, specialized technology and industry, providing an encompassing social structure through all the basic institutions we know in our own civilization rose ghostlike up out of the arid wastelands. Writing and record keeping wove the fabric of society into a unified and enduring form. The archivists of the time furnish us with many invaluable details of their life and times but the overriding focal point of the Sumerian social order was the "gods" and their history. The orientation of their sense of history may be characterized as that of a people dealing with a known past. The overriding motivation was that the past must be studied and understood so that those lessons might be applied with maximum benefit in the present. E.A. Speiser gives a summary of their attitude toward and view of history by listing the stages that a Sumerian scholar living in the second millennium B.C. would have given.

> 1) The beginning of civilization; 2) The Deluge; 3) The crisis under Etana, the shepherd; 4) The rivalry between Kish and Uruk, culminating in the clash of Agga and Gilgamesh; 5) The period of Sargon and Naram-Sin.
> . . . What was the consensus about them?
> 1) Civilization was a gift from the Gods who vouchsafed it to mankind as a full-grown product. It was abroad from the day that "kingship was lowered from heaven" . . .
> 2) After a hazy period of enormous length the gods saw fit to regret their gift to mankind. They sent down the Deluge, which all but swept away the last vestige of life on earth. For a number of anxious days the future of life and civilization hinged on the fate of the precarious craft that bore the hero of the cataclysm; his ark contained, providentially, "the seed of all living creatures," including "all the craftsmen."
> 3) The fresh start marked the beginning of an unbroken chain in which the present was but the latest link. (It meant much the same thing to the ancients that the dawn of history means to us.) Shadowy outlines of

The theme of historical change caused by theological offense is prevalent throughout Mesopotamian history.

---

postdiluvian rulers appear on the distant horizon. The first realm to become manifest is the city-state of Kish. And the first of the new rulers to be featured by historic tradition is the shepherd Etana.[3]

From the time of Etana there are a succession of rulers, some form of government by assembly, an unquestioned understanding that the local "god" owned and controlled literally everything and the king was only a foreman of that "god" who could and would be removed or banished if he did not do exactly what he was told to do. The theme of historical change caused by "theological" offense is prevalent throughout Mesopotamian history. On the other hand, there is a strong sense of continuity and uniformity in the Sumerian view of history because everything could be anticipated since it was all a matter of either doing what the local "god" ordered or not. I include them in the Western framework since they are the earliest source in that context, representing the attitude and orientation of the Middle East and the West until the time of the Greeks.

The high culture and civilization and record keeping of the Egyptians was centered on the deeds of their kings rather than on the events of the past and history as written, careful records of commonplace things was not a priority with them although they referred to the past accurately in terms of the events centering around the "gods." Yet, from the time their civilization arose, there have been records, no more or no less accurate than modern records. Carefully kept lists of rulers recovered stretch back very far in time, recording accurately the succession of human kings and queens preceded by, in the case of the Egyptians, a list of demi-gods, preceded by a list of gods. Western historians often state that the Egyptians were not really interested in history. It is much more accurate to say that they were not interested in history in the same way as the Greeks and modern Western historians and take that as a clue to an understanding of that in which they were really interested, viz. the gods, demi (half) gods, and kings.

The Greek culture, relatively young compared with the Egyptian and the Sumerian, had yet another orientation. They recorded and recounted the events and deeds of the heroes and gods of the past yet their approach was characterized by a spirit of free inquiry, a tendency toward the analytical and the critical. It is generally agreed that the current concept of history as "knowing by inquiry," investigation, was invented by the Greeks although they freely admitted that their sources were usually Mesopotamian. From a

Over centuries, for the Western mind nurtured in the Judaeo-Christian cultural context, history began where the Bible began.

---

slightly different point of view their orientation to an investigative mode was the result of a removal in time and an obfuscation of events that forced them to pursue information in a way not necessary for those who were familiar with it in earlier times "when the living past was an abiding reality." The Greeks were a relatively new cultural force and they were awed by and respected and learned from the much older Egyptian culture and history as well as that of their Mesopotamian sources. Both the Greeks and the Romans have been criticized by modern scholars as deficient as historians because they saw politics as the prime moving force underlying historical change and did not take into account the interplay of material, economic forces. From another perspective, however, the social-political control over the economic arena may have been much stronger than modern historians project. By the time of the Greeks and Romans the view of man and history had moved away from the "god"-centered view of remote antiquity.

With the coming of Christianity, however, the orientation and attitude of the West toward history changed radically. If it is the Greek window through which we view the past, it is the graffiti of the subsequent times' religious gang wars scrawled thereon that obscures our view and turns it into a clouded mirror. Over centuries, for the Western mind nurtured in the Judaeo-Christian cultural context, history began where the Bible began therefore the concept of pre-history, the era of the pre-historical, was a contradiction and the reality of a previous high civilization either preposterous or blasphemous. Shotwell summed it up succinctly

> Christianity dropped all this rationalist tone of the Greeks and turned the keen edge of Greek philosophy to hew a structure so vast in design, so simple in outline, that the whole world could understand. History was but the realization of religion—of various religions, but of one, the working out of one divine plan. It was a vast, supernatural process, more God's than man's.... History has only one interpretation. Rome—city and empire—is the spoil of the barbarian, the antique world is going to pieces, all its long heritage of culture, its millenniums of progress, its art and sciences are perishing in the vast, barbaric anarchy: why? There is one answer, sufficient, final—God wills it. . . . There is sin to be punished. The pagan temples of the ancient world, with their glories or art shining on every acropolis, are blasphemy and invite destruction. Philosophers and poets whose inspiration had once seemed divine now seem diabolic. Those who catch the vision of the new faith, shake off the old world as one shakes off a

**Only forty years ago the curriculum at Cambridge still equated
ancient history with that of classical Greece . . .**

dream. Talk of revolutions! No doctrines of the rights of man have caught
the imagination with such terrific force as these doctrines of the rights of
God, which from Paul to Augustine were clothed with all the convincing
logic of Hellenic genius and Roman realism . . . In Christianity, the story of
nations, of politics, economics, art, war, law—in short of civilization—
culminated, and ceased! . . . For a thousand years and more it was the
unquestioned interpretation of the meaning of history . . . it has been
greater than the interest in scientific history, at least until recent times.
Religion has supplied the framework of our thought and the picture of our
evolution.[4]

To set a perspective, it comes as a surprise to most modern minds to learn
that in 1654, the same period in which Harvard University was granted a
charter, modern musical harmony and modulation had flowered, and Japan
was already beginning its modern development, people could seriously
accept the setting of the date of the Creation of the world, with which the
Bible opens, at 4004 B.C. (on October 26th at 9 A.M.) by the Irish Protestant
bishop, James Ussher. (Annales Veteri et Novi Testamenti)—working with
calculations originally done by Martin Luther on the exact time of the
crucifixion of Jesus, and corrected by Johannes Kepler the astronomer. That
was state-of-the-art scholarship only three hundred plus years ago.

Only forty years ago the curriculum at Cambridge still equated ancient
history with that of classical Greece, that of the Middle Ages with the rise of
Christianity, modern history with that of Europe. It was only the efforts of
Spengler and Toynbee that finally began to cure the myopia of a
culturalcentric perspective.

Although dissent and philosophic and theological opposition to established
Christianity sprung up from time to time and gradually became established
in Europe and the Middle East the critical break with the Christian
interpretation of history came with the development of scientific geology.
The time required for geologic events to occur began to reset our concept of
the age of the earth and then of the solar system and brought into serious
question the traditional teaching on the time of the beginning of the world.
The weight of this geological evidence, written in the rocks and mountains
and ancient seabeds was too substantial to be ignored. Reinforcement
gradually came from the science of biology which contributed a wealth of
details concerning the life of extinct flora and fauna, the fields of

The critical break with the Christian interpretation of history came with the development of scientific geology.

---

anthropology and paleontology which began to identify and trace the ancestry of animals and man back into remote time and the refinement of dating methods that could be applied to artifacts and bone. And so a curious thing happened about a hundred years ago. At the same time that the approach to history in Western culture settled into its familiar form and the interpretations of the politics, the economics, the conflicts and the leading personalities and trends of the modern world began to proliferate, our interpretation of the ancient past was radically challenged. The archeological evidence included detailed recordings of events described only synoptically in the Bible and written three thousand years before it existed. The Old Testament section of the Bible came to be seen as an accurate recording of history and was further reinforced by discoveries related to details that it contained but which were obscure or puzzling. Over time it was put into a finer and finer historical perspective and the relationship between the Hebrew tribe and the preceding cultures in the Middle East clarified. At the same time the panorama of much earlier civilizations unfolded through the work of shovel and pen. One could assume that this would be sufficient to free the vision of the scholars of the West to approach the information from the past with an attitude conducive to objective evaluation. Unfortunately it took the experts only far enough to remove the domination of the Christian ethos, leaving a great deal of virtual influence and bias. Although historiography moved into what I have called the post-Christian era, a cluster of factors developed or remained that have hampered the resolution until this decade of the final and most basic puzzles unearthed in the Middle East.

Although the material reality and the history of the ancient civilizations could no longer be doubted or denied, the categorizing of the traditions derived from them as myth had become so ingrained in the Western mind and vocabulary that any change in that area came very slowly indeed. If the age of the world in the Ussherian sense had to be corrected by any number of magnitudes well, so be it. Christianity, by now splintered, could no longer risk the bad reputation it had gained dealing with a Galileo or a Jordano Bruno. The Catholic sector tended to adopt a more "enlightened" attitude, began to show an interest in science, and simply absorbed the new information. Some sects simply have traditionally gone to the other

The continuance of the classification of some areas of ancient tradition as myth was abetted by the lack of a sufficient level of technological sophistication.

extreme and condemned any historical analysis of the Bible as either irrelevant or demonic.

The continuance of the classification of some areas of ancient tradition as myth was abetted by the lack of a sufficient level of technological sophistication that would enable scholars to understand and allow the possibility of the elements of those traditions—unknown weapons, technical devices, means of flight, communications equipment, advanced medical and biological techniques, longevity—that were much of the reason why they were assigned to the category of myth in the first place.

Another major factor reinforced the interpretation of the references to the "gods" as mythological; the general acceptance of the theory of evolution by prehistorians. In 1794 Erasmus Darwin issued his *Zoonomia, or the Laws of Organic Life.*[5] Erasmus proposed a general concept of biological evolution but it was Charles Darwin who, in 1859, published *On the Origin of Species by Natural Selection*[6] giving his view of the mechanism by which evolution happened. Henrich Schliemann began to excavate the site he thought was Troy in 1870, just one year before Charles Darwin's *The Descent of Man*[7] appeared. The acceptance by prehistorians and field archeologists of the general concept of evolution caused them, and causes them to this day, to look for a continuous evolutionary sequence of events as they penetrate further and further into the past. The prevalent anticipation of a generally more primitive state has, at one extreme, fostered the use by prehistorians and others of such terms as "savagery" and "barbarism." Those projections, focused on the predecessors of the earliest civilizations we know has, at least, made it easier to assign any reference to the "gods" as myth—don't "savages" and "barbarians" always deal in myth?—and made interpretation of the actual findings more difficult. This rationale has encouraged the use of "comparative anthropology," an attempt to understand ancient cultures by comparing them to present day cultures assumed to have the same degree of development. Unfortunately the concept of comparative anthropology when applied has all too often led to "the savage and us" syndrome. The assumption that there is a continuous, unbroken line of evolution from the most primitive hominid through homo sapiens, the beginnings of "savagery" coming with simple tool use, has shown itself to be as detrimental to the work of the prehistorian as it has been beneficial when directed to the ancient civilizations. At worst, it has clouded the question of

It is a bit paradoxical that the theory of evolution has turned out to be an obstacle to the prehistorian.

---

the origin of homo sapiens by causing prehistorians to *preclude* what has turned out to be the real answer. It is a bit paradoxical that the theory of evolution, certainly never a comfortable companion to Christianity and a major factor in easing its grip on Western thought, although opening up vistas in the past in general, has turned out to be an obstacle to the prehistorian.

When the process of historiography is analyzed three main components are discernible. There is the basic factual content, the methods by which those facts are obtained and processed, and interpretation with its various filters of expertise, biases and attitudes. All of these elements have gone through fundamental changes over time. The Judeao-Christian dye in the fabric of Western culture coupled with the residual early misguided assumptions of the natural scientists and prehistorians has perpetuated until the last decade a fundamental flaw in the process of interpretation in Western historiography.

The end result of these mutually reinforcing factors is that the prehistorian even in our time can assign the sober and constantly reiterated claims of the Sumerians that the "gods" were humanoid beings living in proximity to and among them, to whom they could speak, write letters, and from whom they could receive letters and spoken instructions, etc. to the classification of myth—without apology, reason or risk of peer criticism. This erroneous picture of prehistory, because the prehistorians assume an uninterrupted evolutionary progression of pre-hominids through humanoids, is of "savagery" followed by "barbarism" followed by an agricultural society eventually giving way to civil-ization, a citification so to speak, (Latin: *civitas*=city). The evidence from the archeological digs tends to get interpreted within that framework and even what is sought or anticipated from the digs is conditioned by it. As a consequence every civilization or culture discovered is assumed to have a predecessor from which it developed. That principle, logical with regard to the accepted evolutionary premise, is firmly embedded in the thinking of the prehistorian at this point in time. It obviously is an easy step from that position to the assumption that the humans of a civilization that flourished 6000 years ago were obviously very primitive, less evolved than we, and therefore dealt extensively in myth and fantasy. Even an iconoclastic thinker such as Stephen Jay Gould, arguing for "Darwin's evolutionary perspective" and against theories of "scientific racism," "innate

There is a growing sense of unease among the experts centered around the Sumerians.

criminality," "killer apes as ancestors, innate aggression and territoriality, female passivity as the dictate of nature, racial differences in IQ, etc."[8] (contemporary myths?) never questions that premise while taking aim at the forms of biological determinism he finds unsavory.

But, not too strangely, parallel to that attitude and position is a growing sense of unease among the experts centered around the Sumerians. It has been called the Sumerian problem. The question Where did the Sumerians really come from? How does a full-blown, high civilization suddenly appear without any obvious preceding civilization providing the time and place to develop the institutions, the traditions, the knowledge and the science and engineering to produce it? To say that it has become the preoccupation of the prehistorians of the Middle East is almost understatement.

But, almost from the time that archeological collection and then systematic study began in the eighteen hundreds, there have been voices raised in dissent from the mainstream of archaeological theory and opinion. The voices have ranged from learned to bombastic—a near-perfect parallel to the spectrum of consenting voices. The dissent has been based on two dominant factors: contradictions and physical evidence, i.e., unanswerable questions and ooparts. Ooparts is a term invented by Rene Noorbergen, a thorough-going documenter of the factual basis of the school of dissent, who wrote in 1977 in *Secrets of the Lost Races*

> For the past thirty years, there has been a steadily increasing number of historical and archaeological discoveries made at various sites around the world, which, because of their mysterious and highly controversial nature, have been classified as "out-of-place" artifacts—thus the name ooparts. The reason for this designation is that they are found in geological strata where they shouldn't be, and their sudden appearance in these layers of ancient dirt has baffled the minds of many a trained scientific observer. They emerge from among the remains of the treasured past sans evidence of any preceding period of cultural or technological growth. In many cases, the technical sophistication of the ooparts extends far beyond the inventive capabilities of the ancient peoples among whose remains they were discovered.
>
> There is little doubt that these artifacts are also out of place in *theory*, for in no way do they conform to what is accepted as a part of the [mainstream theory of the] development of the human race.[9]

Scientists, especially in NASA, began to interpret events in the Bible as involving advanced technological devices rather than supernatural events.

The quote expresses very succinctly the nature of the two part argument advanced by the school of dissent. The positive counter explanations offered as a result of this alternative view have followed roughly a path of development parallel to that of the mainstream theory. We should see the subject at hand in perspective in that there is a classic pattern of rife speculation at the beginning of any subject which first becomes discernible, usually provoking a predictably contemptuous reaction on the part of the academic world, bringing out its worst aspects often in *ad hominem* attacks (Pyramidiots, etc.) then provoking the interest of some of the more open-minded scholars, and finally becoming well enough defined with sufficient accumulated data that even the "experts" feel secure getting involved—and then often taking all the credit themselves. It is true that there is always a radical fringe involved, especially in such an open field but it is enough to trust the process of attrition by fact that inevitably occurs. Although there have been many persons associated with each stage of crystallization of the alternate explanation, it is convenient to identify each stage with the name of an individual who represents it best.

As is so often the case with individuals who advance radically new ideas, Von Dainiken, perhaps the most well known of the dissenters, has been the center of intense controversy but that is irrevelant to the matter at hand. His book and movie *Chariots of the Gods* is the best example of the way he has traveled the world and collected the examples of mysteries of architecture, land drawings etc. What is important is the fact that, although his conclusions were not specific and accurate enough due to lack of critical information he did call our attention to sites and ruins which forced consideration and reevaluation and stimulated popular awareness worldwide.

The second stage may be defined as the Chatelain stage after the head of the NASA Apollo project communications division, Maurice Chatelain. This stage characterizes the involvement of the scientist becoming interested because the technology that he was involved in forced attention to ancient reports that suddenly could make sense in the light of the latest advancements in his field. Chatelain was especially struck by the sophistication of astronomy and mathematics he found in the ancient texts. Other scientists, especially in NASA, began to interpret events in the Bible as involving advanced technological devices rather than supernatural events. This stage was most important not so much because it lent scientific

Our libraries and museums are now in possession of over five hundred thousand pieces of such artifacts, drawings and texts.

respectability to the subject but primarily because it was the beginning of the time when our technological achievements began to let us understand ancient recorded phenomena as the use of hi-tech devices. This proved to be a crucial factor in the development of the next stage.

The Sitchin phase is marked by the culmination of thirty years of research[10] resulting in a master synthesis based on nothing but the archeological evidence, showing the origin of the suspected extraterrestrials to be from our solar system, explaining the creation of man as a hi-tech genetic engineering process, revealing the nature of the "temples" and ziggurats and pyramids and generally correcting and making precise what had been previously only inaccurately guessed. Our libraries and museums are now in possession of over five hundred thousand pieces of such artifacts, drawings and texts. The scholarship and linguistic abilities that Sitchin exercises on this material form a solid foundation for the conclusions he has reached and the facts enable him to untangle the knots of previous scholarly dilemmas and mistakes.

Sitchin's conclusions may be summarized using a paraphrase of the statement of objectives made in his prologue. Using the Old Testament as an anchor, and **submitting as evidence nothing but the texts, drawings, and artifacts left us by the ancient peoples of the Near East,** he proves that Earth was indeed visited in its past by astronauts from another planet just as the ancient peoples themselves believed that superior beings "from the heavens"—the ancient "god" or "gods" came down to Earth. The Nefilim, mentioned in Genesis, whose name in the ancient Sumerian translates correctly to "those who were cast down upon earth," were an advanced race who landed here approximately 450,000 years ago to set up a colony with the purpose of mining gold. The pictograph sign, term, for the lords in the Sumerian ("god" or "gods" was not in their vocabulary) was a two-syllable word: DIN. GIR. It can only be translated as "the righteous ones of the bright, pointed objects" or, more explicitly, "the pure ones of the blazing rockets." There can be no doubt that they were "living beings of flesh and blood, people who literally came down to Earth from the heavens."

He identifies the planet from which these astronauts came as an additional member of our solar system now being searched for by the Naval Observatory, astronomer Charles Kowal at the Palomar Observatory, and searched for by the NASA planet probes. Sitchin demonstrates that the

There can e no doubt that they were "living beings of flesh and blood, people who literally came down to Earth from the heavens."

ancient texts plainly show that this planet is larger than the earth, orbits the sun once every 3600 earth years in a direction opposite that of the other planets, passing through the region of the asteroid belt in its closest approach to the sun and then moving outward in an extended elliptical orbit far beyond Pluto. He deciphers the sophisticated ancient cosmology that explains better than our present sciences how Earth and other parts of the solar system such as the asteroid belt came into being. He lays bare ancient reports of a celestial collision, the result of an intruding planet being captured into the Sun's orbit in the very early stages of development of our solar system, and shows that all the ancient religions were based on the knowledge and veneration of this twelfth member of our solar system since it was recognized as the home planet of the Nefilim, of the gods. He proves that this Twelfth Planet was the home planet of the ancient visitors to Earth and submits texts and celestial maps dealing with their space flights to Earth.

He describes them and shows how they looked and dressed and ate, glimpses their craft and weapons, follows their activities upon Earth, their loves and jealousies, achievements and struggles, unravels the secret of their "immortality."

He traces the dramatic events, an actual revolution of the lower echelons of the Nefilim who were fed up with their onerous mining tasks which forced their geneticists to engineer a creature to take their place, that led to the "Creation" of Man, and shows the advanced methods of genetic engineering by which this was accomplished. The first attempts combined the genes of a number of animals with those of homo erectus and the results were generally bizarre and frustrating; the results also indirectly gave rise to a part of what has traditionally been considered mythology, tales of creatures that were sometimes strange combinations of very different animal and hominid characteristics. Finally the decision was made by the Nefilim to combine their own genes with homo erectus and we were the successful product. They apparently had advanced skill because they were able to control and predict the sex of the individuals produced. The first successful creatures were called Adaba in the Sumerian—the Adam of Genesis. He then follows the tangled relationship of Man and his deities, and throws light on the true meaning of the events passed to us in the tales of the Garden of Eden, the Tower of Babel, the Deluge, the rise of civilization, the three branches of Mankind.

Finally the decision was made by the Nefilim to combine their own genes with homo erectus and we were the successful product.

The Garden of Eden tale in Genesis is a condensed version of detailed accounts in Sumerian texts of how Man, when first "invented," could not procreate as is the usual case with mutants; how that ability—"knowing" in the sense of "Adam knew his wife"—was given to us; how the genetic experiment, as a result, got out of the Nefilim's control leading to the expulsion of the new creatures "to the east," the outback, out of the area where they were kept as slave-servants, the area reserved to the Nefilim.

Over an extended period of time, our ancestors acquired knowledge, skills, experience and eventually began to copy their masters the Nefilim. The Tower of Babel tale is, again, a condensed version of the historical episode concerning the discovery, by the Nefilim, of the fact that men had gone so far as to try to duplicate one of their rockets—we do not know, in detail, how accurately—to the extent that the Nefilim agreed that, if men could progress that far, they could do, eventually, whatever they really set their mind to do. As a result the Nefilim deliberately brought about a divisions of languages, on the basis of divide and conquer or, at least, control effectively.

The story of the Deluge marks a point when the Nefilim had become so dissatisfied with the experiment, because of the proliferation of the new creatures, that they were ready to destroy all Men. The evidence shows that the Nefilim were apparently aware, as we have only recently learned in theory, that the Antarctic ice sheet could build up an underlying slush layer that would allow it to slide into the ocean under the influence of a sufficient disturbance. They resolved that, when their planet returned to the vicinity of Earth again causing a strong perturbation of this planet, they would let the ensuing flooding destroy all humans. It is possible that, if it were not for one of them, Enki, who was sympathetic to the humans, who secretly instructed Noah, one of his favorites, in the construction of a craft this book would not be written, and you, dear reader, would not be around to read it. We came very close, at that point, to extinction.

Sitchin then shows how Man—endowed by his makers biologically and materially with "instant" civilization, knowledge, and science as a result of a deliberate choice to preserve Man as a useful tool after the Flood—ended up crowding his gods off Earth. He shows that Man is not alone and that future generations will have yet another encounter with the bearers of the Kingship of Heaven.

We have been the way we are now, almost from the beginning

We have been the way we are now, almost from the beginning. The only general characteristic that seems to have developed gradually in our nature was the level of self-consciousness. But after that limitation was transcended we seem to have exhibited the basic nature we have now. In this lies the solution to the puzzles surrounding the disappearance of Neanderthals and the sudden appearance of modern man. We were civilized from the beginning—at least those of us who were kept in the areas where we served the Nefilim. This fact throws our evolutionary development and our history into a totally different light. No matter where we find man we find culture, sometimes regressive sometimes advanced, but always an easily discernible culture. If we examine the period 6000 years ago we find civilization in a remarkably full blown form with every institution we now count as modern. If we look backward to the stone age we have been conditioned to anticipate only the crudest and rudest glimmering of humanity—and we find instead a level of artistic sophistication and dress closely resembling our own and so on into the past. The traces of our existence has a twofold character; there is the well defined evidence of the cities and the more elusive evidence of the migratory groups. The real picture most closely resembles a gradual worldwide migratory dissemination of humans who had appeared on the planetary scene quite suddenly, from centers of civilization—cities, the sites of which we now realize were far more ancient than we could have believed a short time ago—showing clear traces of cultural, traditional and artifactual similarities either as a remnant of or copy of the parent centers. The causes of the expulsion from those centers we now know and that expulsion was the impetus for the worldwide pattern of migration. To cross the Atlantic and encounter humans was only to meet ourselves coming from the other direction. Those who were driven into the outback when we became too numerous probably did not fare as well— there is both archaeological and documentary evidence of regression in some cases—but the expulsion did give rise to the migrations that spread humankind over the globe and did create a situation which engendered a greater independence. The forced separation also set the stage for the eventual overrunning of the city-states, the centers of civilization by the "barbarian," out-back tribes. The pattern of psychological maturation is clearly different from the process of evolutionary change and I examine that fact in the following chapter. We may have been "growing up" but we were

We were intentionally deprived of certain advantages from the beginning and systematically repressed.

never less than we are now and we have been that way for much longer than was recognized by the experts until only a short time ago—and yet that span of time is only a period of 350,000 years.

We were intentionally deprived of certain advantages from the beginning and systematically repressed. Longevity was a characteristic of at least some of the first humans. There is mention of some of the more notable ones living a relatively extraordinarily long span of time although the human life span has stabilized at a shorter span over time. But the Nefilim enjoyed a tremendously extended or perhaps indefinite life span and they were able, according to the records, to bestow that benefit on humans if they so wished. And, for the most part, they did not. Only a few cases are mentioned.

The recovered documents attest to the fact that the Nefilim, once humans had acquired sufficient technical skills, became quite concerned about their ability to control the rapidly multiplying groups. The Tower of Babel story, well known from the Old Testament, is found in much greater detail in the Sumerian histories. When the Nefilim became appraised of the fact that humans were attempting to duplicate a rocket (the tower was probably the ziggurat type of launching pad they used) they were threatened enough by it to actually create a diversity of languages, apparently on a basis similar to the way India imposed an official language in the recent past. The diversity of languages was imposed on the principle of divide and conquer—or at least control more effectively. Even today, nationality, that primitive divisive factor in human society, is associated with language. Instead of the seemingly incredible interpretations traditionally put forth about the events of Babel it is clear that the Nefilim were simply taking very pragmatic action relative to their own interests. The effects are still with us.

The Nefilim did not hesitate to attempt to keep us under control after we had attained self-procreational abilities, by disease starvation and oppression. The fact that the Nefilim could vote to literally wipe us totally from the face of the earth, as they did just previous to the Flood, shows quite clearly how they viewed us, even then, from their perspective. We enjoyed a status equivalent to that of an animal used for experimentation in our labs today—perhaps not any more status than a chimpanzee—though we had reached a level of technological competence that was far beyond the primitive state of Homo-erectus.

There is a clear pattern of cyclical infusion and decay of technological and cultural traditions.

There is a clear pattern of cyclical infusion and decay of technological and cultural traditions. Sitchin has pointed out the 3600 year cycles that correspond with the return of the planet Marduk which are marked by a surge in information and technology followed by a period of gradual decline. Rene Noorbergen's study of ooparts points up this fact with striking examples but it is also very important to differentiate between the documentation of the existence and use of certain technology by the Nefilim and the existence and use of certain technology by our ancestors. The former invented it and the latter copied or used it.

A major factor leaps at us from the pages of the Old Testament; the gulf between the maker and the made in all respects permeates the words of the writers of that history. If there is an almost infantile awe in the tone and attitude toward the makers it is quite logical. Until we gradually acquired the ability to procreate ourselves—in the long term a critical advantage but in the short term almost the cause of our extinction before we were established—all of us were made through the services of official "birth-goddesses" in laboratory conditions. We were invented and used specifically for menial, servile work as slave-animals.

It is interesting, however long the separation in time, that there is evidence of a universal cult of the Great Mother (usually associated with the sign of the moon) found in many variations throughout the world. This would seem to be a product of an ancient tradition which recognized the source of human nature in the experiments of the chief geneticist of the Nefilim, a woman, Ninhursag.

Even after the Flood when the decision was made to let us continue in existence, the relationship was one of total subservience. So it is not surprising that the Nefilim were looked up to as all-powerful and awesome. They possessed technology and weapons which we did not even understand and they held the power of life and death over us absolutely—and they were motivated by emotions, principles and politics that are very much like the ones which we are familiar with in our world today. To grasp the level of consciousness operating there, we have only to reflect on the repetitive, irate ranting that the Nefilim master of the Hebrew tribe carried on (I am the Lord, YOUR god and you shall not put strange gods [my brothers or cousins] before ME) at a time when humanoids were in short supply and the Nefilim vied with one another for the valuable slaves.

We should not be embarrassed about the naivete that we have exhibited collectively over centuries.

Sitchin's synthesis of the information from archaeology, history and the Old Testament unites the mainstream interpretations with that of the dissenting school of thought simply by correcting the deficiencies of each. By doing so he has provided the perspective needed to envision part of the new paradigm to which the indicative arrow of history's interpretation points. The breadth and detail of Sitchin's work can only be summarized very briefly here; there is much to be gained by a thorough study of his writings. Although the implications of his work are perhaps not fully realized yet, I predict that his work will have the relative impact in time as Darwin's *Origin of the Species*.

The significance of the evidence presented by Sitchin, should be immediately overwhelming. Yet the fact that its ramifications do not seem apparent to many persons exposed to them is a classic example of how widespread conditioning and programming can seriously cripple human thought. Any evidence that the Bible is anything other than what the varous religions based on it claim it to be is rejected *a priori*. Any major contradiction of the prevailing doctrine concerning our direct evolution from prior anthropoid forms tends to be rejected by the scientists most concerned with that theory as well as the proponents of the various theories concerning the even earlier evolution of life on earth and where it came from. Astronomers and geologists and astrophysicists who have laboriously worked out theories of the beginning and evolution of our solar system tend to react negatively to a gratuitously given, detailed account of the actual historical facts of that development. But, as with any new information, we can only hope that everyone will approach it with an open mind and that their private context will not be too threatened. But think about it: have we not been telling ourselves for some time that the real story could be that way in our science fiction? Have we, indeed, not been projecting a hope of such discovery—Tillich has called it our "ultimate concern"—as if from some deep source in our collective unconscious? Is it not beyond coincidence that when the facts are made known we recognize something startling yet strangely very familiar as if almost programmed in our genes . . . ?

We should not be embarrassed about the naivete that we have exhibited collectively over centuries; if it were not for the fact that we have reached the level of technology we now possess we would probably be in the same position. It is critical to appreciate the fact that unless we had attained a grasp

**An important historical event on a medium size, ordinary
planet orbiting an ordinary star located in the outer regions of
an ordinary galaxy.**

of the fundamentals of genetic engineering, of rocketry and space flight, of
geology, of the nature of our solar system etc. as we only recently have
acquired them, and reached the level of scientific achievement we now
enjoy, we could not even have understood the real nature of the events
about which Sitchin is writing. He has succeeded in slipping into place the
last pieces of the puzzle of human origins, setting in proper perspective, once
and for all, an important historical event on a medium size, ordinary planet,
orbiting an ordinary star located in the outer regions of an ordinary galaxy:
our creation as a species and a race. Since the event involves all of us
intimately we call it important; in the overall perspective of the universe it is,
most probably, relatively trivial. It also seems reasonable to allow the
possibility that we, being the successful and enduring product of a planetary
experiment, may be something of a curiosity to whatever beings are capable
of studying or learning about us. The interest, on the part of whatever
imaginable or unimaginable entities could simply be curiosity that makes us
a local tourist attraction or it could be a more serious sociological study. It is
even more reasonable to assume that there is an ongoing observation and
monitoring of this planet by the Nefilim, providing that their race has not
met with some catastrophic disaster.

At the beginning of this chapter I noted that it is necessary to reexamine
the psychology of our views of history. Even in light of the impressive
evidence it would be folly to think that acceptance will come easily in what,
in a slightly different context, Stephen Jay Gould has called the "hardest of
all games to win."[11] But why?

Since the information has been available from the beginning and actually
given to, at least, those of us who were able to understand and record it, it is
not as if we had to mentally evolve to a certain point in order to grasp the
facts. The question may be asked then: why was the knowledge lost or
misinterpreted? The answer is that it has not been lost but it has been
misinterpreted. It is not as if we were not told; the records and the
information were available from the beginning. Once the decision was
made to allow us to continue in existence we were given civilization, social
forms, detailed information about the formation of our solar system,
advanced astronomical techniques, the details of our history and creation,
technology and science, foremen (kings) to act as representatives of the
makers, structure enough to go it alone. The decay of the knowledge is easy

Since we ourselves are a large part of the proof itself there is an unique solipsistic web which is difficult to escape.

---

enough to understand; the time spans are great, our individual lives are relatively short, information is distorted through ignorance, breaks in the tradition due to natural catastrophes, the less desirable motives of individuals, the power plays of official castes, vested interests and the petrification of institutions, the destructive force of superstition, bestial regression, callow indifference. But we can now see clearly that the major factors that have influenced the current western view of the real nature of the "gods" and our beginnings are the influence of the Judaeo-Christian tradition, the reliance on literary history in the past, the acceptance of the theory of evolution as a continuous process by the prehistorians, the drawbacks of comparative anthropology, the deliberate suppression of non-conforming evidence, the lack of technological knowledge that would allow us to understand the phenomena described in the ancient texts.

As modern and enlightened as we now consider ourselves, we still have a blind spot that is reinforced by those same deeply ingrained attitudes of the past. This pervasive shadow of innocent bias is paradoxically most manifest in the position of those very scholars whose concern is elucidating the way our attitudes toward pre-history and history have evolved over time. The Western mind, particularly the Western academic mind, as a result of these cumulative influences, has a deeply set schizoid attitude toward the idea that a more advanced race could have come here, even if only from another planet in our solar system, and genetically engineered our species. Yet there seems to be an enormous market for even the most contrived stories of that type in the rag press. (Researching the subject requires wading through the seediest of intellectual swamps to even identify the real landmarks.) Almost everyone is fascinated by the concept, says that, in light of the constantly accruing evidence, it seems plausible and reasonable. Even after careful differentiation from the subject of flying saucers, the occult and associated material, there doesn't seem to be any way a person can fit it comfortably into their everyday thinking. There is an elusive something that seems to run even deeper than the typical "scientific," religious or popular reactions of the past to the claims of a Galileo or a Pasteur. There does not seem to be any depth or weight of rational or scholarly evidence alone that could change that set. Certainly, since we ourselves are a large part of the proof itself, there is an unique solipsistic web which is difficult to escape. It does not seem to be simply a matter of it being just too amazing to be believed. It

It is an awesome sight to witness an apparently well balanced, mature scholar and/or seasoned scientist metamorphose right before one's eyes.

---

does seem, however, to be no less than some strange taboo to be overridden only by an expansion of awareness. It certainly is cultural. Westerners should at least understand that much of the rest of the planet does not have that problem or share that attitude.

A recent event illustrates the peculiarity of our attitudes very clearly. When one of the Viking landers returned a photo of what seemed to be a pyramidal structure and a face-like object in a stretch of desert on Mars it was motivation enough for two computer scientists, Vincent DiPietro and Gregory Molenaar, associated with NASA's Goddard Space Flight Center, to use computer enhancement to study the images intensely. Their conclusion that the symmetry of the objects raised a doubt that nature could have been totally responsible obviously implies the plausibility of the existence and presence of some intelligence at some time on the surface of Mars. Although two NASA engineers and Mars experts, James Oberg and Harold Masursky disagree with the theory of Richard Hoagland, a science writer, that the topographical features in the proximity of the "face" and pyramid represent the traces of a city's streets, neither denies the possibility that intelligent beings could have existed there at some time. Experts at MIT's Artificial Intelligence Laboratory, Bell Labs, Lucasfilm Ltd. and the Earth Satellite Corporation which analyzes Landsat images were all enlisted, under the title Mars Investigation Group, to study the sixteen selected images. Regardless of the conclusions they draw, (positive, from preliminary reports)[12] the assumptions involved are extremely significant. Here are the top experts in the field investing precious time on muddy photos of limited resolution requiring sophisticated computer enhancement to determine if the images in question may be the work of intelligent beings *on the surface of Mars* when we repeatedly witness so-called open-minded scientists reject the extensive information from the archaeological digs right here on our own planet out of hand without even bothering to inspect the data—many times on the basis of their *a priori* conviction that no evidence, regardless of what new facts or new plateau of expertise it was built on, could exist in the first place. It is an awesome sight to witness an apparently well balanced, mature scholar and/or seasoned scientist, on mention of the subject, metamorphose into a poisonously defensive religious sectarian, an irrationally waffling cynic, or a harried, peer-group-pressured individual right before one's eyes.

What is implied but seldom acknowledged is that myth and legend are such partly because the deeds and implements and weapons spoken of seemed fantastic even for the culture of our recent past.

The crippled state of our educational system contributes little to any extensive, accurate understanding of important events in our past for the ordinary student. Any person making an effort to achieve a comprehensive overview of our ancient history, however, will immediately be confronted with a wealth of information clearly showing that the scholars of the past spoke of the gods as a matter of literal fact, and made a clear cut distinction between the obviously imaginary folk myth (giant animals that carry the earth on their backs etc.) and the tales of humanoid personages doing hi-tech deeds. We merely have to substitute hi-tech for mysterious, advanced for supernatural, to see it as they did. We are the ones who stand in danger of the second meaning of superstitious, maintaining a notion despite evidence to the contrary.

The standard academic treatment of the subject is based on the premise that all legend and myth have roots in the simple-mindedness of primitives awed by the phenomena of nature, becoming more complex over time, and then somehow civilizing their religions by giving impetus to the worship of and the building of temples to the "gods." What is implied but seldom acknowledged is that myth and legend are such partly because the deeds and implements and weapons spoken of seemed fantastic even for the culture of our recent past—and therefore had to be imaginary. The usual answer to the fundamental question why is there a world wide phenomenon of "legend" and "mythology" in the first place is the same given to the even more pointed question why is there a startling universality of recurring themes running through the traditions of all cultures wherever one finds them on the planet. The simplistic standard answer is that it is due to the commonality of human nature—it has even been ascribed conversely to a "poverty" of imagination!—and the basic need of all men to seek answers to the same questions about the unknown. But even the perceptive high school student will immediately question the extreme coincidences apparent in the similar themes. As a single example, creation stories are often in two parts; the creation of man and then a second creation after a devastating natural disaster—usually a flood—somehow tied to humans incurring the anger of the gods, the new era often due to the survival of a human pair, animals, etc. The parallel with the Sumerian history of Utnapishtim (Noah in the much later Hebrew condensation) is obvious. It has been pointed out that the word in Chinese for the original ancestor of men, who overcame a

phenomena as the science fiction of the primitive mind is simply no longer a viable or tenable explanation.

great flood, is a phonetic sound that approximates very closely to the word Noah. Noorbergen points out that researchers have uncovered thirty flood legends in the Orient, forty-seven in North America. The peoples of Polynesia, even the remote Orinoco Indians, and the natives of Borneo, all hold the story in memory.

The memory-catching rhymes and cadences of poetry, an exquisitely tuned method for transmission of traditions in the aural mode for millennia, gave way to a prose form when writing became prevalent. It is probably difficult for us to appreciate how much of an innovation this was considered. The inquisitive, say-it-like-it-was approach to history blossoming among the Greeks around 600 B.C. found natural expression in this mode. The first historians among them working in the prose genre are generally considered to be "protohistorians" by modern scholars, not because of their competency or methodology so much as because of their subject matter. Hecataeus of Miletus, a sophisticated and discriminating Greek scholar, one of the earliest pioneers of this mode had no use for the popular level tales of the past and went about sorting out the truth as he saw it—even complaining that the popular stories were "ridiculous." Yet, because he was preoccupied with the family trees and genealogies of the great "mythical" families of the Middle Eastern ancient past, he is treated condescendingly by modern scholars. This is an excellent example of the biased rationalization to which every student of ancient history is exposed in the guise of scholarship. It takes the form of an amusing contradiction in the attitude toward the teachings of the ancient historians and philosophers whose writings are still known or available to us. This attitude is particularly apparent in the standard academic approach to acknowledged intellectual giants like Aristotle, Plato, Pythagoras, Democritus, to name only a handful among the Greeks, or the enlightened rulers of ancient Sumer. On one hand those philosophers, whose thought, thousands of years ago, encompassed nearly every problem—and solution—that we know today are at once recognized as intellectual giants of integrity yet, when they speak of the history that had gone before them, are made out to be naive, even simple. Those rulers and their archivists and scribe historians are accepted as sources when they speak of men and dismissed when they speak of "gods." Because our set is to call anything mentioning the "gods" "myth," their mention of the "gods" must, in our eyes, be the product of primitive imagination. Those Greek historians who "corrected" myth the scholars accept. Those who discriminated

There is a startling universality of recurring themes running through the traditions of all cultures.

---

between popular stories and the valid history of the "gods" are rejected. Even the illustrious prehistorian, Gordon Childe, is at his worst when he makes gratuitous statements like "The gods, **being fictitious**, . . . "; "At Lagash the several deities worshipped by the citizens were **imagined** as related like the members of a patriarchal household." We do not listen; we project. The traditional approach to myth and legend that considers those phenomena as the science fiction of the primitive mind is simply no longer a viable or tenable explanation.

A careful analysis of the historical facts shows that the scholars of ancient times had a great deal more accurate information available to them than most historians have judged and the scientific traditions preceding them were of a much higher level. Far too often the negative judgements of the modern prehistorians concerning the competency and accuracy of the information possessed by their ancient counterparts is based on *a priori* assumptions or convictions of the impossibility of the validity of that information. The real primitives, history shows, were those power players who deliberately destroyed such priceless storehouses of ancient knowledge as the great library of Alexandria or the museum at Heliopolis. The wanton destruction of the vast Alexandrian library, paralleled only by the systematic destruction of the Central American historical-cultural records by the Spaniards, may well be a major cause of our loss of authentic knowledge of our origins. The recognition of the significance of that knowledge, by those responsible for the obliteration of thousands of precious documents, only reinforces the fact that there have been conscious efforts to distort or obscure the tradition.

When we examine the tradition of other great cultures of the world it is striking that there is a very significant common theme that forms the underlying fabric of ancient traditions throughout the world.

The preoccupation of any of the scant histories to be found in the ancient culture of India is with the deeds of beings, recognized as superior, in a past golden age. Scholars in the west, unable to interpret that information as anything else but mythical because it seemed too fabulous to be believable, have been unable to understand the real meaning and significance of it.

It is often noted that the Chinese have the oldest and richest continuous recorded cultural tradition on the planet. The Chinese were already doing archaeological digging and studies in 200 B.C.—a time which Western culture considered ancient up until recently! Chinese historical orientation

The shared, transcultural preoccupation with the "gods" and their deeds and politics obviously transcends the category of coincidence.

in the past is characterized by a preoccupation with genealogies and reverence for the ancestors and a past golden age which was looked on as a model to be imitated. Certainly the attitude of China towards its history, manifesting itself in a proprietary attitude of the government with regard to the records for many centuries, is somewhat different from the general orientation of the west but this is only because we in the West tend to judge by comparison with ourselves and do not listen just as we do not when it relegates those ancestors to the category of legend and myth without any real attention to the understanding of the Chinese concerning that subject.

As we have seen above, the Greeks had a tradition of "gods" in their past and the Egyptians based their entire civilization on that reality.

Although it is often noted that all of the major cultures, and, indeed, most of the cultures of the earth, considered the deeds of a class of real superior beings, who had inhabited the earth as **the most significant events of the past** scholars, because of the pervading bias, fail to ask **why**. The shared, transcultural preoccupation with the "gods" and their deeds and politics obviously transcends the category of coincidence. When we ask the questions why should it have been this way in the first place? why should there be this huge tradition of flesh-and-blood-larger-than-human-type people with advanced technological devices in our planetary history? we can say that it was the "science fiction" of the primitive mind but do we see anyone bulding a temple like that at Baalbek to Captain Kirk or Mr. Spock? One of Sitchin's contributions is to demonstrate that, although given different names by different cultures, the same Nefilim individuals were involved in the various cultures' traditions. The difficulty scholars have found with this view is alleviated when we realize that the Nefilim lived, if not indefinitely, at least for thousands of years. No valid reason is ever advanced by historians or prehistorians why, at the same time we take the king lists as valid and accurate, the list of gods is rejected as myth.

It is a surprise to many modern minds to learn that, for millennia, the peoples of the world were not interested, for a variety of reasons, in the history of the world that lay in the distant past much less in the details of the life that humans led in those times in the same way that we are. An oral method was usually used to hand down the important traditions of an individual group but the purpose was predominantly utilitarian; when written records were kept history tended to be official history. As can be

Recognition of the true nature of our origins gains us a principle of unification of the entire planet. That principle is the concept of generic humanity.

seen from the above, the orientation of other cultures toward history is not ours, but neither is ours a criterion. The preceding paragraphs summarize the general consensual position of the experts concerning the orientation to history of the major ancient civilizations but it is easily forgotten that a scholar in the past time in the west would not have felt free to state such opinions and probably would not have held them even privately anyway.

The resolution of the puzzles of our history ultimately shows that the contributions of both the mainstream and dissenting school of thought concerning the nature of the "gods" and the real nature of the events of the ancient past are invaluable. The tremendous amount of information and analysis done by the field archaeologist and supporting experts, the brilliant decipherment of lost languages, the scholarly detective work of the mainstream scholar provided the broad basis of hard fact so essential to the subject. The prodding of the school of dissent has been just as positive a contribution, forcing the resolution furnished by Sitchin in an elegant, scholarly and dispassionate synthesis of both. Everyone involved turns out to be partially correct, a characteristic revealing itself in every phase of the reexamination and reinterpretation carried out in this book. The final paradox may be that the real solution may suit neither!

But, after a short span of history, we still exist. The Nefilim are not here on this planet at least in any obvious mode—yet we will have to get used to the fact that we are part Nefilim. We have made enough progress in our own independent development to have reached a point where the facts dealt with in this book can be understood in sufficient perspective so the author does not feel that his fate automatically will be that of Giordano Bruno. At this writing *Newsweek* carries articles on the newest work by physicists on not just the fourth dimension but eleven potential dimensions. A major theme of a current major science fiction movie is the positive expansion of consciousness by chemical means. The grand unified field theory is probably within our grasp. But we have problems that are far reaching and complex. If the planet is on hold it is due to the residual historical patterns of philosophy, religion, politics, education, science, social forms and values that we have espoused collectively and individually. The major objective of this book is to sketch the ways in which we can begin to gracefully and intelligently replace those old ways with a clear and fresh vision. We should certainly be careful of making the vision into another

We shall "be as gods" and attain to relative immortality but in a mode which will be of our own doing.

"religion" from the start. The perspective afforded us by the overview of our beginnings, giving our history a coherent and elevated meaning, should be welcomed with relief by intelligent persons. It frees us to take our place in an ongoing process in an aware and conscious mode rather than a blind and groping one. It integrates our past with our present and our future; inevitably we "shall be as gods" and attain to relative immortality as they did and humbly—but in a mode which will be mostly of our own intelligent doing unless, perhaps, we receive some assistance directly from them. The possibility of future contact with our makers seems quite probable but, due to the independence we have achieved, our relationship with them will be a major determinant in the future politics of our development.

The dominant message of this book may be re-stated simply at this point: recognition of the true nature of our origins gains us a perspective sufficiently encompassing to be able to reevaluate all of our past history, customs, institutions, attitudes and differences and, in doing so, to realize a principle of unification for the entire planet. That principle is the concept of generic humanity.

The readjustment of our perspective is mirrored in a natural adjustment of jurisdiction among the academic disciplines. Because we have been civilized from the literal beginning of our existence, our "evolution," now still seen against its roots in natural evolution but understood as an unique rapid metamorphosis, becomes our **known history**. That history, **now a context rather than a puzzle** and integrated into our present, together with archaeology becomes a **sociology**. That extended sociology becomes an expanded context for our psychology. The liberated character of that psychology allows it to become again the integrated context of the entire spectrum of all phases of our minds' activities including transcendent experience, philosophy, and science now understood as generic functions of our inherent philotropism. The sciences expand so that re-search acquires a new dimension since there is evidence of technology and information in the ancient records that may be worth much to us in the present.

In the following chapters I sketch the outlines of the new conceptions of evolution, psychology, sociology and then draw the framework of a planetary paradigm based on those conceptions and analyze the trends in our thinking that can now be clearly seen to anticipate that fulfillment, that paradigm, not just in an improved way of doing things, but in a new

The point of critical-mass of information about our unique genetic creation and who we really are is inescapably upon us. The last pieces of the puzzle have fallen into place.

definition of what humanity really is and who we really are, **the creators of our own reality**.

We may have been able to remain blase to the fact that pioneering archaeologists have repeatedly uncovered the physical reality of cities and civilizations that formerly were considered to be only the content of legend or myth; previously, may have been able to hold in skeptical suspension our judgements concerning the reality of gods, demi-gods, kings and dynasties and high cultures the sophistication and frequent splendor of whose material remains and records now lie in our museums for all to witness; may have been able to previously marvel, without drawing conclusions, at the stupendous feats of monumental engineering and organization written large across now remote or barren landscapes, been awed, in unresolved puzzlement, over the contradiction of mature law, trade, education, travel, economics, and advanced medicine, science and technology clearly evident in remote times the scholars have insisted were primitive; may have been able to labor as students and scholars, docilely submissive to the righteousness of "authorities," naively viewing the bulk of the history of the world previous to the Greeks as somehow the irresponsible and unreliable figments of innocent, ignorant, even primitive peoples probably somehow less human than ourselves; may have been able to sidestep the multitude of discovered artifacts, ooparts whose tangible logic speak eloquently of our predecessors as technologically and socially like ourselves rather than the grunting savages the cloistered savants would have us believe; formerly taken refuge from the responsibility and risks of personal education and evaluation behind the robes of ecclesiastical or institutional dogmas acknowledging as unquestioned inspired authority the very texts parts of which were claimed to be the product of less developed minds and to be taken metaphorically; formerly, been able to leave to the "experts" the explanation of the gross inconsistencies of our species' developmental patterns when viewed against the known sequences of previous species; capitulated to the hive pressure not to judge for ourselves what we could glimpse over the academic and religious barriers. But our racial childhood is now over and we are coming, typically reluctant and turbulently, out of our racial adolescence faced with the responsibility of self-determination and mature action. The point of critical-mass of information about our unique genetic creation and who we really are is inescapably upon us. The last pieces of the puzzle have fallen into place.

CHAPTER 4

EVOLUTION OR METAMORPHOSIS?

To call the current situation we find ourselves in, as a race, with regard to the fundamental questions — where did we come from — what are we —what is our purpose — where are we going — a puzzle is an understatement; for those who have considered it in any depth it is a dilemma of the first order. The disagreements are not about details and fine distinctions; the disagreements are about the fundamental issues and they are radical.

The theories and doctrines and opinions advanced as to how biological organisms and we, as a special case, came to exist on this planet range through the following.

TRANSMISSION THEORIES

Directed Pan Spermia: the theory, advanced by Crick and Wickramasingh, that says that molecular compounds, of a level of complexity and specificity that would eventually engender living organisms under the right conditions, tend to be disseminated throughout the universe and "seed" any environment, planet or otherwise, that can sustain them.

Self-Causality: self-transmission from a higher level of consciousness.

SPECIAL CREATION THEORIES

Creation or mutation at a distance by sophisticated information transmission by an advanced species located somewhere else in the universe.

Creation by an advanced species that visited here and interbred with primitive hominid types.

Creation by a supreme cosmic being of infinite omnipotence as exemplified by the traditional interpretation of accounts related in the book of Genesis in the Bible.

EMERGENCE THEORY

Development through indigenous evolution on this planet beginning from inorganic sources once the planet had reached a point that would support it, the process being driven by either purely mechanistic physical laws or an inherent universal potential for consciousness.

Development through pure chemical chance as a beginning leading to random evolution.

In the recent past, however, the information regarding our beginnings has developed to an entirely new dimension, a point of critical mass.

The most cursory of inspections shows the disparity between these various theories. Attempts to synthesize two or more of them do little or no good.

It may be argued that we have at hand, due to the diligence of the Leakeys in South Africa and many other throughout the world, a body of information that seems to impressively reinforce the emergence type of theory along the lines of Darwin's evolutionary doctrine. Yet a statement of that type will bring the Bible-based thinker out of the chair quoting chapter and verse to show that the evolutionary theory is just that and not supported by the Bible which he feels is the statement of ultimate authority.

It may be argued that a developing species such as we, gradually becoming more conscious and knowledgeable over time, should perhaps not be expected to know the details of our actual origin since we have not been around that long. But it is immediately apparent that that type of reasoning presupposes an evolutionary context in the first place.

It seems quite clear that where there is that much latitude for discussion and debate there is a puzzle of the first order.

In the recent past, however, the information regarding our beginnings has developed to an entirely new dimension, a point of critical mass.

What is fascinating about the situation is the fact that almost everyone who has previously advanced a theory about our origins has been partially correct.

The Bible turns out to be extremely accurate history. What is true about the bible-based thinker's belief is that the Bible contains revelation; what is inaccurate is that the revelation came from a supernatural being; it came actually from a creator that was humanoid but technically advanced. The history it details had to be revealed since newly invented creatures would have no way of knowing of the events that brought them into being. The bible based thinker must come to realize that it is not a matter of argument between two different interpretations of scripture. It is the source of that authority itself that must be understood in a new light.

Those holding to the theory of pan spermia may be found to be correct in so far as primordial molecules of amino acids, recently identified in interstellar space, may give rise to DNA that may disseminate throughout the universe. The explanation why there is only one genetic code rather than many on this planet seems best explained, however, in terms of the

Evolutionary progression was interrupted at the point of homo erectus, with the deliberate intervention of the Nefilim.

formation of the earth through the collision with the satellites of the invading planet, allowing for a seeding of planetary proportions. Though possibly correct in general, the theory of Pan Spermia is incorrect insofar as it does not take into account the interruption of the linear process of evolution through artificial manipulation in our case.

Those holding the theory that an advanced race landed here and interbred with hominids or homo erectus are very close to the actual fact yet incorrect in that the inception of the race was through artificial means of biological engineering rather than physical intercourse. Those holding this theory usually base their position on the enigmatic passage in Genesis that says explicitly that the "sons of the gods became enamored of the daughters of men." The ancient records bear out in detail the literal truth of that statement but the intermingling of the species did not occur until after the genetic creation of man, and after man had developed the ability to procreate and had somewhat stabilized as a race. The attraction of the younger male Nefilim to the new female humanoids and the resultant dilution of their racial strain was a major cause of their decision to destroy us.

Those theorizing that we, as a race, might have been self-created by a process of transmission from a higher level of consciousness at least partially parallels in a curious way what actually happened in that the Nefilim were certainly of a relatively advanced level of evolution and did indeed self-transmit through the use of their own genes but the transmission was physical rather than on the level of pure consciousness and the event was strictly in our usual space-time dimension.

The proponent of the evolutionary theory is correct in that the evidence shows that early forms of hominids preceded Man; but the information available in the ancient records show that the evolutionary progression was interrupted at the point of homo erectus, with the deliberate intervention of the Nefilim, by genetic manipulation. Many of the enigmas of paleontology are thrown into a new light because of this information and the relatively absurd velocity of human evolution is explained. The vehement objections of the religious or the erudite or the sensitive that we were selling ourselves short by seeing ourselves as only an upscale ape were instinctivey correct but contextually erroneous. Those who accepted the concept but were

The popular scenario of biological evolution on this planet is of a linear, progressive development and adaptation of a species in the direction of greater flexibility and more intelligent interaction with its environment.

---

reluctant to assume responsibility for its direction instinctively sensed that there was something incomplete about it, something more to know about the mechanism before they felt licensed to drive it. A prevalent characteristic of those who were able to espouse and promote the concept of linear evolution unreservedly has been their strong, almost paradoxical, sense of being able to transcend it, a futant trait that gave them a self-confidence to proceed even though they might not have all the evidence. The new perspective adjusts and completes all those contexts in a way that amazingly vindicates all those positions.

The popular scenario of biological evolution on this planet is of a linear, progressive development and adaptation of a species in the direction of greater flexibility and more intelligent interaction with its environment. But, even at this point in time, there are two general interpretations of how the process operates.

Richard Leakey gives an excellent summary of the current situation in *The Making of Mankind*

> Darwin's notion was that new species came about through the gradual addition of new features to an existing species, so if one examined the population at one point in time one would see the full characteristics of the parental species, while subsequent examination, perhaps a million years later, would reveal a related but distinct species, displaying new features. And at any point in between, there would be transitional stages with the new characteristics still incompletely developed. The evolutionary transition, he argued, ran throughout the whole species population. This theory has been given the imposing name of **"phyletic gradualism."**
>
> . . . The opposite theory, which proposes evolutionary change through relatively rapid periods of modification, separated by long periods in which the species remains unchanged, does allow for some transitional forms, but it does not demand the existence of a long series of very finely graded intermediates as with phyletic gradualism. In this view of evolution, known as **"punctuated equilibrium,"** the anatomical change would be complete in ten or a hundred generations, and this transitional phase would be very short by comparison with the species' total duration. This explains the failure to find fossils of intermediate forms . . .
>
> These, then are the two theories; a slow population-wide transition

It is startling enough that man should not have appeared for another two or three million years—instead of some 300,000 years ago.

---

between one species and the next, or a brief evolutionary spurt separated by a long period without change.[14]

In view of the gradually accumulating evidence (Napier and Clube, etc.) furnished by astrophysics concerning the collision of comets, fireballs, and meteorites with the earth over the entire history of the planet, some of which are of such size as to cause hemispheric devastation and the extinction of species, the most comprehensive picture of evolution must also include this variable.

The gradually accumulated evidence from the Leakeys' and others' work in South Africa, the finds made in Java, Sumatra, China, the Middle East, Siberia points to the same type of linear development in the evolution of the prehominid and hominid species. Once a species appeared on the scene the time spans for the development of that species, from inception to the fullest exploitation of its potential, are measured in millions of years. A striking characteristic of all species preceding us, including homo erectus, is the extremely modest progress made in cultural and other developments even over those millions of years. Compared to our progress it seems as if, even for homo erectus, there was almost none. The stone toolkit for homo erectus, Acheulean tool technology, remained the same for at least 1,300,000 years.

It is startling enough, as Sitchin and various experts have noted, that Man, if the normal time pattern seen in the sequence of succession of previous hominid species held, should not have appeared for another two or three million years—instead of some 300,000 years ago. Working with only the information we have from paleoarchaeological finds, as has been pointed out by Dobhansky, there is not even a real progenitor for us in the fossil records. But the nature of the evolutionary development that Man has exhibited since our sudden and too early advent is even more startling.

But the historical evidence clearly states that, although there is solid evidence that the natural progression did, in fact, eventually bring about homo erectus, the Nefilim directly interfered with evolution at that point and used homo erectus genes to combine with their own in order to create us as slave-animal that would be both sufficiently intelligent and docile to serve their purposes for menial tasks.

The Nefilim directly interfered at that point in evolution and used homo erectus genes to combine with their own in order to create us as a slave-animal.

From the point when the Nefilim decided to allow us to exist after they had attempted to destroy us through the mechanism of the Flood and gave us "crash" courses in civilization to the flights of the space shuttle is only a matter of some thirteen thousand years. A comparison of the progress we have made in that relatively brief period with the millions of years it has taken other species of hominids to stabilize and progress relatively far less is startling to say the least.

It is necessary to digress here to recognize the objection that any comparison between technologies as such can be very misleading. It is certainly true that one has only to examine the culture of the hunter-gatherer groups of the Kalahari to recognize that a people using only the simplest of technologies and tools may have a rich cultural life and a profound knowledge of their environment because of their actual physical needs. But what is involved here is the radical dimension of innovation and exploration due to mental development and expansion over relatively very short periods. We do not see evidence for that in the culture of homo erectus or any other hominid species known to us. We do see it dramatically in ourselves.

The speed, indeed the acceleration, of our progress can only be seen, against that background, as absurd. Measured by either the norms of a continuous or discontinuous type of evolutionary process a serious question is raised as to whether our kind of progress should be classified as evolutionary process in the usual sense at all. Certainly it does not resemble the slow, adaptive, selective molding of a species over millions of years, once it has appeared on the scene, that we read in the paleoarchaeological records. Neither does it match the gradual process of emergence of a species filling a vacated ecological niche after a catastrophically destructive event. It does resemble the learning process of the maturing child who is rapidly retracing neurological processes. It does have the character of full blown suddenness. It certainly resembles the process of metamorphosis beyond the point of metaphor. I propose that the key to this phenomenon is our bicameral genetic heritage; what we are witnessing, indeed experiencing, is certainly an adaptive and selective process at base **but the greater part of the human experience, by far, can only be understood as the effect of the rapid ascendancy of the Nefilim genes.** An analogy with the Calculus is apt here;

The greater part of the human experience, by far, can only be understood as the effect of the rapid ascendancy of the Nefilim genes.

our anomalous developmental velocity has, as its second derivative, the accelerative component of the advanced gene set's potential.

It is obvious that genes code for intelligence. That the genetic code builds more and more complex brains, with greater scope and synthesizing power, is taken for granted. But once a new model (species) has appeared, however, the records show little evidence that there is any obvious or inevitable radical upgrading of intelligence within that species. Cultural evolution is the working out of the potential created by a neurological revolution (like plugging a new chip into a computer adding a function that it did not have), the advent of a new species with a new capability for intelligence. The manifestation of that new level of intelligence over time is too often interpreted as a cause rather than a result of the advent of a new neurological capability. For homo erectus to change, in some geographical areas, from a non-symmetrical to a symmetrical shaping of hand axes has been the basis for theorizing about even the language capabilities homo erectus might have possessed. Unequivocal evidence for the refinement of a tool making technique needs no other explanation than the fact that the species under study possessed the potential to achieve it in the first place. These remarks are not intended as an argument for the punctuated equilibrium theory of evolution; the objective is to point out a pervasive mind set that causes a misinterpretation of the evolutionary process.

Since we have been ignorant of our unique beginning, we assume that we are a linear continuation of the evolution of hominids; that is the current, generally held paradigm—by at least those who can accept evolution in the first place. Even at this point in time, however, there is no strong position among the experts.

> The hominids labeled H. erectus, "archaic" H. sapiens (including the Neanderthals) and "modern" H. sapiens **probably** represent a continuum, and the patterns of change within these lineages represent . . . microevolution. **Nevertheless**, some of the most interesting paleoanthropological work concerns the last great step in human evolution: the shift, about 45,000 or 40,000 years ago, from archaic H. sapiens to modern H. sapiens.
> (David Pilbeam, Ph.D., "The Descent of Hominoids and Hominids," *Scientific American*,[15] (emphasis mine)

Our attempt to map our developmental patterns into the overall picture of hominid evolution simply warps our perception of the entire pattern.

The result of our current thinking is that we tend to ignore the radical anomaly of our unique situation and project our experience backward in our evaluation of the evidence concerning the development of previous hominid species. Our attempt to map our developmental patterns into the overall picture of hominid evolution simply warps our perception of the entire pattern. The recognition of this process for what it is opens up many areas for reconsideration.

We should separate ourselves from the progression of hominid species up to and including homo erectus. The divorce, paradoxically, may not be easy but that simple change of perspective will immediately show us that normal process of evolution, subject to the usual pressures and influences on the organism, may be learned from the fossil records and actual observations of existing species undergoing change just as we are doing now—but that the patterns are indeed very gradual, take a very long time, and the changes in any individual species even over millions of years are mild to say the least, being a little more noticeable, perhaps, as with homo erectus, if the species under study is higher on the relative scale of intelligence. The term "paleocultural" has been coined by Arthur Jelinek of the University of Arizona to differentiate the prolonged stability in morphology and behavior manifest in all species preceding us from our rapid cultural progression.

A secondary, but important part of the differentiation between us and our predecessors on the evolutionary tree are some noteworthy physical characteristics. A relatively naked skin rich in sweat glands, a turned down nose, an unusual head and large brain, a cleft shaped depression in our upper lip, a system of laryngeal muscles that allow us to use a very complex communication system of sounds are all unique. In the context of our bicameral heredity they become very significant and research should be carried out to determine precisely the contribution or combination of contributions from both sides which determines each one. A beginning in this kind of research would undoubtedly lead to another level of work with subtler features, eventually producing a detailed genetic analysis of our makeup.

State-of-the-art paleoanthropological technique combines the fossil evidence with anatomical data, developmental studies and molecular

The new perspective provides a key to the nature of the transition from archaic H. sapiens to modern H. sapiens.

---

analysis to form a judgement about a specimen or a species. The detachment of our case from the preceding linear sequence of species should implement those techniques by creating two distinct contexts of study. We still exhibit many characteristics that should be studied by the existing disciplines and the adjusted perspective will facilitate those studies.

Whether the theory of phyletic gradualism or that of punctuated equilibrium will prove out over time to be more accurate depends on the evidence for transitional variations in species. The few significant finds that can be considered in that category are within the timespan and context of modern man. The transition models in the Middle East, the Skhul and Qafzeh people, and the finds in the Omo Valley, Laetoli and Border Cave are more understandable—we were invented to take the place of the lower echelons of the Nefilim in their South African mines—perhaps elegantly demonstrative, in the context of our genetic creation. They would otherwise remain pawns in the debate between the proponents of the "Neanderthal phase" theory (Man originated in and spread from the Middle East) and the "Garden of Eden theory" (Man originated in and spread from Africa). Again the ancient records show that almost everyone is partially correct. The new perspective provides a key to the nature of the transition from archaic H. sapiens to modern H. sapiens which David Pilbeam pointed out as a major area of investigation in the above quote.

We now know that the first of our kind were produced by biological engineering, not mating, and the gestation was provided by officially appointed "birth-goddesses," Nefilim females assigned to the task. The records also say explicitly that, once we were given the ability to procreate, eventually there was ordinary sexual activity between humans and Nefilim—indeed the dilution of their racial purity because of this was the primary reason for their decision to destroy us—as well as between humans and humans. It seems reasonable to assume, therefore, that, eventually, there was also procreation between individuals of all degrees of human and/or Nefilim lineage. There conceivably could have been procreation between humans and homo erectus. Reflection on these combinations shows the variety of genetic proportions and features that would carry down to our time, the knowledge of which would provide potential maps

In this context the inaccuracies of both the theories of phyletic gradualism and punctuated equilibrium as the mechanism by which evolution works can be corrected.

for genetic researchers concerned with differentiating them. Against that background occurred the expulsion of unwanted humans (grown too numerous for the work requirements through the acquired ability to procreate) into the "outback." What have been called "regressive" types of humans may be seen, in this context, as the possible result of having been expelled into more primitive conditions where they had to fend for themselves with little technological knowledge or experience. The ancient records clearly state that, when first created, we drank from the ditch and ate the grasses with our mouths. That suited the purposes of the Nefilim well enough since they really only desired a slave-animal but a human of that level of development and self-awareness most probably would not develop a high culture. The details we have about Enkidu, the "wildman of the steppes" who became a friend of Gilgamesh are valuable clues. Primitive before being literally civilized (citified) in a short period of time, he seems to epitomize the "regressive" outcast human type. The transitional models from Skhul, Shanidar, Qafzeh and other finds fit easily into that context once we have adjusted to the separation of ourselves from the previous sequence of evolution. In this context the inaccuracies of both the theories of phyletic gradualism and punctuated equilibrium as the mechanism by which evolution works can be corrected. We can approach the construction of a theory that applies to all species at all times with a fresh outlook having been freed of the unconscious pressures to skew it radically, indeed grotesquely, to accommodate the incongruities of our specie's unique situation.

But the best specimens, by Nefilim design or by genetic probability, were, or rapidly became, far more developed than that and already showed a dominance of Nefilim hereditary traits. It appears clear from the records that the Nefilim tended to keep the better specimens. Obviously there would be a greater chance that those who were kept would mate with other humans and even Nefilim than the outcasts who might even have mated with homo erectus. Since the potential existed for the superior specimens to appear, however, some of those pushed into the outback and eventually migrating throughout the continents would have been capable of forging and sustaining a higher culture. This is the key to the understanding of the puzzles presented by the advanced art and traces of sophisticated astronomical knowledge and technology found in very ancient sites. It is the key to why

We do not know exactly how much of a "budget" product "the Adam" represented—and that uncertainty can be quite disconcerting.

rudimentary to high culture is always found where humans are found no matter how far back we trace ourselves. Half of the puzzle of ooparts, "out of place" (only in the context of the old interpretation) objects in history, is explained in this context of human cultural development. The artifacts were not out of place; our understanding was simply not correct. The information gathered by Von Dainiken and Chatelain finally takes on clear and logical meaning and is set in proper context. Both have acknowledged the conclusiveness of Sitchin's synthesis. The other half of the puzzle of ooparts is explained by the fact that some actual traces of Nefilim technology may have survived. The entire area of archaeological and historical re-search and analysis becomes one of the most significant human endeavors and should be given the highest priorities. Archaeology becomes the textbook of human Sociobiology 1A.

In perspective, the Nefilim geneticists had to experiment a good deal, failed in their attempt to produce a satisfactory cross of homo erectus and animals genes, and seemed to have been, at that time, perhaps a little in advance of where we are now in genetic engineering. By that criteria, they were approximately 350,000 years ahead of us. One may easily speculate that the Nefilim were unable to predict what the intellectual evolution might be of an artificially created, genetically bicameral species of this level of complexity even though it is explicit in the records that they could predict and control the sex of a fetus. When they produced a physically satisfactory and mentally competent model they called it Adapa (the Adam in the later Hebrew), the first perfect one. And that, apparently, was good enough. We do not know exactly how much of a "budget" product "the Adam" represented—and that uncertainty can be intriguingly disconcerting.

Only part of our genetic background was originally geared to the environment, time, circadian and biorhythms and genetic imperatives of this planet. The other half is the product of a planet on which a "year" is probably 3600 times as long as earth's and which passes far beyond Pluto in its outer orbiting and is driven by a different set of genetic imperatives. It is no wonder we exhibit the often conflicting characteristics that are perhaps unavoidable in such conditions at this level of complexity.

And it is quite clear from the ancient records that we may, literally, be affected by a "budget" approach taken by the Nefilim since they were only interested in a slave-animal with specific practical characteristics. There

The basic postulate here is that cross-seeding between the two planets due to the recorded collisional events in the early solar system was the cause for the compatibility of the coding.

were a number of duds before the first satisfactory model was produced. It is at least reasonable to assume that subtler intellectual faults, conflicting psychic characteristics or genetically based diseases, any of which did not effect basic performance or product life to an unacceptable degree, would probably have been passed over.

In view of the level of technological skill possessed by the Nefilim and the details of the information about our creation described in the ancient texts, the following scenarios may be projected as to their intentions and actual success in the project

1. They intended and accomplished a straight-forward, genetic cross using the highest level technology they were capable of at the time and produced a product that satisfied their expectations and needs and which was as genetically perfect a merging of the two codes as they could accomplish.

2. They deliberately manipulated the structure of the coding of the two strains, producing a stable product that was also modified farther for traits such as docility and subservience, resistance to disease and physical endurance. Gold and diamond mining are very stressful occupations and, even today, miner-candidates are screened for endurance under high temperatures in the South African mines.

3. They possessed enough advanced genetic knowledge to even modify the coding to program us to respond to external command cues of some sort. These could be visual, verbal, electromagnetic etc. Although it may seem an extremely far fetched possibility to some of us now, all indications are that our capability to do precisely that level of engineering will be available to us soon in the future.

In the science of genetics, although we have only recently begun to make breakthroughs in this area and have been able to read the entire genetic coding of only the simplest of organisms, there are certain facts that we have learned. The coding of our genes contains intermittent sequences of what the geneticists call "junk" genes, lengthy sequences that are apparently meaningless. It seems worth investigating whether those sequences might result from the merging of two very complicated and different codes and whether those sequences might indicate an imperfect or incomplete

We have only to look in the mirror to find a subject who can tell us exactly what it is like to be the product of genetic engineering . . .

melding. It is not inconceivable that there might be an element of inherent incompatibility between the two codes. The basic postulate here is that cross-seeding between the two planets due to the recorded collisional events in the early solar system was the cause for the compatibility of the coding but the separation over a lengthy period of time under different conditions may have allowed some differentiation leading to partial incompatibility.

It certainly seems reasonable to assume that, if there were the possibility of partial incompatibility or incompleteness, then genetic defects could result. At any rate we have only to look in the mirror to find a subject who can tell us exactly what it is like to be the product of genetic engineering—in our terms—before we have reached a point where we might attempt the experiment ourselves on our level of complexity.

Genetic science currently lists identified human genetic diseases well into the thousands. I propose a systematic sorting of the known genetic diseases and any subsequently discovered to determine which are caused by obvious identifiable external agents such as exposure to radiation for example and those which might have their origin in the bicameral programming which, under certain circumstances, might issue contradictory or conflicting instructions. The most valuable clue might come from evidence garnered in the course of paleoarchaeological evaluations of signs of pathological conditions in recovered skeletons. If a genetic defect can be traced back as far as the very beginnings of our unique species it would be quite significant.

It is possible that the percentage of the race, at any given time, that is afflicted with incapacitating insanity, serious or fatal diseases, handicapping neurosis is far too high compared to a species that evolved naturally. We have no way to make comparison in this case. To approach the investigation of the genetic causes of these serious afflictions with our bicameral uniqueness in mind is not without merit and systematic scientific investigation of the topic seems worthy.

Reflection on the entire context of insanity in this perspective immediately brings to mind the persistent association of insanity with creativity; an overbalance of the advanced Nefilim genes creating a conflict with the imperatives of the more primitive set of homo erectus? Or simply an individual regressive variation of the physical neurological system that cannot stand the strain of the imperatives of the advanced set?

It will be easy for those so inclined to see here the root of the "war"

It is essential to establish a perspective on immortality from the beginning.

---

between flesh and spirit that pervades so much of the Judaeo-Christian tradition in a variation of the dreary attitude of pessimism that either sees man as intrinsically "evil" or in need of salvation. But the new paradigm negates the view in two ways: the authority invoked by the Judaeo-Christian tradition is the Nefilim master who had a very personal, even selfish, interest in declaring certain items or actions taboo, i.e. reserved to himself—rather than a cosmic Intelligence. Although it would only take one to prove the case, there have been and are many individuals who have dealt with the full spectrum of human consciousness, human potential, in a positive and magnificent way. At this point in time our concern is not how to maintain our sanity but how to achieve relative immortality as quickly as possible in keeping with the fullness of the dignity of the heritage we possess.

The records and history are clear about the consequences of genetic inheritance from the beginning. As a general principle, a human aware of being parented by a Nefilim father or mother felt entitled to privilege. A single well known example is that of Gilgamesh who knew that his father was a human and his mother a Nefilim female. As a result (two-thirds divine, one-third human) he considered himself entitled to the longevity and/or relative immortality enjoyed by the Nefilim. The history of his seeking that gift is well known. What he obtained was a gift of a plant which would give him longevity but not immortality—and, when it was eaten by a reptile of some sort, he became discouraged and would not return to harvest it again. One loses some sympathy for him at that point in the story. One certainly can recognize the full-blown ruminations about death common even to present day humans in his soliloquies but Gilgamesh comes across as something of a macho, spoiled child of privilege. Hamlet had nothing new to offer, however. The real significance of the history of Gilgamesh lies in the detail it gives us about the status of genetic castes, and the fact of immortality. The knowledge that the concept of castes based on genetic inheritance was familiar to humans from the beginning gives us a starting point from which to reevaluate the entire context of race, caste, royalty and kingship, slavery. But, far overshadowing that insight is the simple fact of the availability of the immortality which we are already seeking. Not only does the new paradigm give us a starting point for the development of the context and concepts for the next profound step in our evolution, the

When Maslow said "Above all we fear the godlike in ourselves" he, perhaps, did not realize the full import of his remark.

regality of relative immortality, but the positive reassurance that it can be achieved—even, apparently, bestowed on an existing human when the requisite level of technology is available.

The reciprocal interaction of the ancient information and our technological capabilities is well illustrated in the case of longevity and relative immortality. If we had not achieved an understanding of the basics of genetics and achieved some proficiency in the mechanics of genetic engineering we would not be able to understand what the ancient texts are saying. When the information does become clear it aids us in being able to see the overall picture and even find significant information that may serve as guideposts for us in our pursuit of the goal of immortality. That information takes the form of a history of a race, the Nefilim, while they were present here, who went beyond a life span that may already have been exceedingly long because of the nature of the environment on their home planet. The information available shows that they were able to grant a human immortality, were quite certainly able to restore a dead person to life (unless they could literally not find the parts of the body as in one case) and that those abilities were not mysterious but simply a function of their technological expertise both in genetic engineering and possibly advanced botanics.

It is essential to establish a perspective on immortality from the beginning. The recognition of immortality as the next profound step in the realization of the fullness of human potential should include a clear awareness of that step, as profound as it certainly is, as one more in our evolutionary progress. It is not just that we will need very long life spans to accommodate to the tremendous distances of space travel, or that the time required to assimilate the enormous volume of information we have available to us in ever increasing amounts will demand a prolonged life to be able to synthesize a meaningful overview of it; it is a matter of dignity.

When Maslow said "Above all we fear the godlike in ourselves" he, perhaps, did not realize the full import of his remark. The concept of human immortality, with its inevitable forcing of the development of a level of technology to restore, even under extremely difficult circumstances, someone unfortunate to be killed accidentally or deliberately, meets with a number of deep-seated negative reactions. The most frequently heard takes the generic form of a rejection based on its stemming from a perverse

We are not absolutely ignorant of how another species of our level of intelligence and consciousness looks and acts and thinks.

---

human pride which is contrary to the "will of God." Translating "god" into "god(s)" or Nefilim makes it quite clear that we are dealing with an ancient and deeply ingrained fear. To seek what was the gods' or to violate a taboo (eating food reserved to the gods, entering territory that was their exclusive preserve, etc.) could bring punishment. If we have lost sight of the real nature of the gods we have not lost our sense of taboo. Immunity to death is only different from immunity to smallpox by degree. It is only reasonable that we enjoy that which our Nefilim forbearers enjoyed through the efforts of our own minds and hands. The recognition of ourselves as more than we have ever thought ourselves to be, setting our own evolution in perspective by detaching it from the linear sequences preceding it, provides us with a touchstone for integrating the developing approaches and disciplines centered on the study of Man. We may never feel completely and easily at home on this planet until we achieve relative immortality and remove the shadow of death's inevitability that can mar our most conscious moments.

"Well damn," you say, "When I look around we don't seem any different!"

But that is precisely the point; you could, and should in view of the evidence, say that what you observe is precisely the way a genetically engineered creature looks and acts and thinks. We need to retool our thinking radically. No longer can we nod sagely at the maxim that in-house wags scribe on coffeehouse menu chalkboards "The problem with human nature is that we have nothing to compare it to." We are **not** absolutely ignorant of how another species of our level of intelligence and consciousness, which has apparently evolved without artificial interference, looks and acts and thinks. The fact is that we have, in considerable depth, the historical details of the way the Nefilim lived, loved, fought, ate, slept, communicated, travelled, used science and technology. Although we may not take the identical direction, that knowledge may be invaluable in making the present and future decisions as to which directions we shall take. The most significant perspective afforded us by the knowledge we have gained of the Nefilim as a race is the nature of their priorities. The state of their technology 450,000 years ago seems very close to the stage of scientific achievement we have reached only in the last decade. It is most profitable to have, for comparison, the choices they had already made relative to their ability to engineer their environment and their physiology. We should

We are just at the threshold of the Genetic Revolution.

recognize that we are now in the final stages of the Industrial Revolution when, having gained the power and succeeded at much, we also have had to recognize, sometimes tragically and painfully, that we can also pollute and destroy as well as improve and so we have begun to fine tune—the aesthetic stage, we might call it. By contrast, we are just at the threshold of the **Genetic Revolution**. If the Industrial Revolution gave us the power to restructure, engineer our environment by many magnitudes relative to the simpler previous technologies, genetic engineering has given us the power to restructure our physiology, body and mind, by many magnitudes greater than anything we have previously known. If the Industrial Revolution forced us to confront basic philosophical questions of values and ethics and morality, the Genetic Revolution will inevitably cause us to face and deal with far more profound questions. The literal ability to design a new human being—for that is ultimately the ability we will shortly possess—virtually total conscious control of our racial evolution/metamorphosis has its Nefilim parallel. It is possible to speculate that their extraordinary lifespan, at least relative to ours, is a function of their planet's orbital period, or orbital velocity, etc. but, on the grounds of the amount of importance they attached to the Tree of Life and the Tree of Knowledge (high-tech, physical, biological entities), it seems more reasonable to look on their longevity as something achieved, and of high priority in their thinking.

Only a short time ago we discovered that we could control our genetic future. It will be some time before we fully grasp and incorporate the profundity of the implications into our habitual consciousness. We will develop a context for implementing that potential much more intelligently and rapidly in the present and the future when we view it against our now known past. The Nefilim had reached that mastery 450,000 years ago and obviously utilized at least some of the potential for themselves personally—as well as practically as witnessed by our creation. In view of the Nefilim example and our own tendencies, it would be easy to say that it is simply "natural" for any advanced race to control their lifespan, to achieve relative immortality. I personally am completely convinced of that "law" already. But the concept, however, will be the subject of philosophical debate from the cocktail tray to the classroom to the laboratory for decades. And the laboratory will be where the answers are determined to a great extent. What we must carefully examine is how much our unique bicameral genetic

We are a unique product of genetic engineering, a mutant species... We are Homo Erectus-Nefilimus

makeup determines not only our biological level of evolution but what we may call our mental evolution. We may be looking at a complex of imperatives; a tremendous potential and an exciting challenge.

Poets and scientists, visionaries and philosophers, explorers and scholars have sensed it, glimpsed it, suggested it but we, thanks to the labor of many scholars and the definitive synthesis of Sitchin, can say it simply and without equivocation; we are **an unique product of genetic engineering, a mutant species** which has reached a relative state of development, both psychologically and technologically, where we can reflexively appreciate that concept of ourselves and act on it. The mutant slave-animal awakes from an ancient sleep, from an amnesia caused by taboo; sapiens unbound and rising. All of our science fiction projections are fulfilled yet cannot match the amazing fact that **we are Homo Erectus-Nefilimus.** We become truly sapient on recognition of the full import of that simple genetic fact.

CHAPTER 5

BICAMERAL GENETICS, BICAMERAL MIND

We have leaped forward in mental evolution in a way that continues to defy self-analysis.[16]

Edward O. Wilson

above all we fear the godlike in ourselves.[17]

Abraham H. Maslow

The facts about the nervous system are too robot embarrassing, too challenging to larval theological and political systems. It is just too early on the evolutionary clock for the species to face the neurological facts, for the robots to decipher their own circuitry.[18]

Timothy Leary

It is startling and mind-expanding to discover that we are the product and possessors of two vast gene pools, a composite physical make-up, a deliberate, highly conscious redirection of two separate evolutionary lines, the merging of two racial "memory banks," collective unconscious, the experience of two planetary histories and traditions. Knowing the nature of our bicameral mind makes the term Homo sapiens sapiens, the doubly wise human, very meaningful. Our psychology is now better comprehended as a manifestation of the rapid metamorphosis we are clearly undergoing. Understanding what that means evolutionarily in terms of our physical make-up comes rather easily; grasping the full implications for a more accurate and profound understanding of ourselves psychologically tends to proceed somewhat slower since we are so "close" to those processes. And mind is the leading edge of our metamorphosis.

Surely one of the most fascinating questions one can contemplate on this planet is Why is it, when *we ourselves are both the investigators and the subjects*, that we seem to not really know what we are and what is the nature of our mind? Just as with the subject of our beginnings, the interpretation of our psychological make-up generates a number of radically differing schools of thought. Whereas the discussion of our origins assumes that our genesis was of a single, albeit strange, creature, any attempt to define or, more

From the philosophical perspective there is a great variety of general viewpoints concerning the nature of the human mind at this point in time.

discreetly, to describe the human psyche inevitably involves a definition of the nature of the creature because we think of ourselves in terms of mind. To describe that area of definition as a wilderness of controversy might still be understatement. The disciplines of philosophy, theology, psychology, sociology and biology many times seem to be seeing an entirely different specimen through their "microscopes."

From the philosophical perspective there is a great variety of general viewpoints concerning the nature of the human mind and its functions at this point in time. What the human mind thinks of itself is the ultimate question preoccupying the human mind at this point in its development.

There are those who see the human mind as a static phenomenon. In this general view the human mind, fixed and complete from the beginning, can acquire information, process it, enrich itself but cannot expand its capabilities, cannot and is not evolving toward a new form.

There are those who think of the human mind as primarily a local and limited manifestation of a higher and more comprehensive consciousness. Some versions of this view would even attribute cosmic dimensions to the field of this super-consciousness. Development and expansion of the human mind, in this context, is usually understood in terms of greater and greater awareness of participation in the dimensionality of this super-consciousness.

There is another group of thinkers who conceive of the human mind in the same evolutionary terms in which they define the entire human being, holding that the human mind is evolving toward an ever more expanded and fuller dimensionality and capability as we both experience and react to and manipulate local conditions as well as actively and consciously explore new areas of perception.

There are those who think of the human being as made up of two distinct parts, body and soul, and that mind is a faculty of the immaterial soul.

Another group thinks of the human being as a purely material being whose mind is a function of the complex biological brain/neurological system.

Yet some others hold that the human mind operates in a continuum of energy that encompasses a spectrum from the purely material-neurological

If we allow the archaeological perspective to enlarge our view it appears that all the major general schools of thought are partially correct.

all the way through the quantum mechanical. A minority of this group of thinkers claims that the most essential operations of the human brain in on the quantum level, speaking in terms of quantum consciousness.

Some say the mind can know an objective order outside of itself; some say the mind can know only its own subjective composite impressions garnered through sensory input. Some say there is an objective order but the mind only knows its subjective synthesis of the sensory input from that objective order.

If, however, we allow the archaeological perspective to enlarge our view it appears, again, that all the major general schools of thought are partially correct when correlated with the augmented history which we now have at hand.

Those who understand the nature of man's mind to be enrichable but not evolving, having the same potential when it appeared on this planet as it does now are correct in so far as we were genetically created with the potential to be as we are from the beginning but this view does not take into account the fact that our bicameral potential drives us to metamorphose rapidly beyond what we are now.

Those who hold that the human mind is a local, partial manifestation of a greater, higher dimensional consciousness are correct in a curious way in that half of our psychological makeup is derived from a more advanced, a "higher," Nefilim genetic base. They also, perhaps, are concerned with an ancient tradition that we shall examine in a later chapter in a somewhat different form. It is possible that the Nefilim, as part of the data base that they imparted to us, included some of their own philosophy, their metaphysics, their ontology, the direction of their future development.

Those who hold that the human mind is an evolving faculty are correct in the same measure as those who hold for evolution in general but are not correct in that they do not take into account the interference with the natural evolutionary process and merging of the two genetic programs resulting in a unique "mind," and a rapid metamorphosis.

Those concerned with the variety of models we have accumulated of our mode of perception and the way they have effected our thinking about the area of epistemology may find a new perspective when they see the manner

We are now able to understand the actual characteristics of human mind, human psychology, from the time we were invented.

in which the criteria we have consensually worked against for so long has been conditioned by or been a product of our traditional and many times erroneous interpretation of our remote history.

In 300,000 years we have come up from our earliest form, the "black-headed ones" eating the grasses with our mouths, drinking from the ditch, going about unclothed to flying the space shuttle, exploring the planets, deciphering the mysteries of quantum mechanics and analyzing the first split second of the expansion of the universe. The expanded context in which we can now envisage that progress requires certain critical adjustments of our understanding of it.

It is imperative that we readjust our thinking concerning the **chronology** of our existence in order to understand ourselves and human mind in the remote past. Although we have been taught to think that there was a linear evolution in which primitive humans gradually evolved to the point where they were able to form fragile communities and then progressed to an agrarian and finally a city environment, we now recognize that we were civilized **first** (lived in the city-centers or mining centers of the Nefilim and worked for them) and then some of us were forced into an uncivilized (non-city-center) environment when pushed into the out-back. Under those circumstances the humans in the city-centers were contemporary with humans in the "wild," in the out-back.

But is is not enough to simply correct the depth of focus of our historical view; we must readjust our thinking, based on the expanded historical context, to the fact that we are now able to understand the actual characteristics of human mind, human psychology, **from the time we were invented** and trace the phases of change we have passed through psychologically until the present. Each phase of our metamorphosis has distinct psychological characteristics.

The expanded context makes clear that there were and are several variables that have influenced the quality and direction of the psychological component of our rapid metamorphosis.

The arbitrary decisions of the Nefilim as to what they would grant us and what they would not genetically and otherwise obviously is fundamental.

The basic mechanics of genetics, heredity, in the determination of our

The mutant had ceased to be the simple servant-child and begun its adolescent period of gradually accelerating self-discovery.

ongoing development is also a critical variable; perhaps the one element that was at least a partial unknown even to the Nefilim.

Sexuality takes on a peculiar significance as a critical element. All indications from the translated details indicate that, when first created we had little self-consciousness, and we were sterile. That was quite precisely the way the Nefilim wanted us; no complications, maximum output, sufficiency intelligent for their purposes which were quite utilitarian. At that stage our development was in the hands of the Nefilim. It is clearly stated in the translations of the ancient records that wisdom was "fashioned" for us; the model was improved by granting us the ability to procreate, the gift of "knowing." Sexuality was given to us so that the Nefilim could have more of us to work for them. The ability to procreate, fundamentally to experience full sexuality was a gift but it was also the first up-leveling of our self-consciousness. (The fact that sexuality was a crucial variable then may give us a basis for the role sexuality continues to play in the process of metamorphic consciousness expansion.) When it was "turned on" by them genetically it activated a dimensionality of consciousness that set us on a path from which there was no turning back. The unique activation was due, apparently, to the level of potential already extant. Then the mechanisms of genetics, heredity, dominance, recessiveness began their inexorable work. The mutant had ceased to be the simple servant child and begun its adolescent period of gradually accelerating self-discovery.

It is intriguing to note that, being at a stage of scientific advancement, 300,000 years ago, only slightly beyond that which we have reached only recently, the Nefilim seemed to not have been able to foresee all the consequences of both that gift and even the long-range effects of the fundamental mechanisms of genetics. It may have been easier to foresee the fact that, eventually, there would be sexual commingling of the species than to predict that the gradual ascendant thrust of their more evolved genes would come to dominate and spur us to more and more rapid self-awareness and self-determination and yet they let the fact that the "sons of the gods became enamored of the daughters of men" grow on them until it was an unacceptable situation.

With the ability to procreate we became numerous, then bothersome—passing over, gradually, to the mode of the active quest for self-determination. We were expelled into the out-back, east of Eden (what

The central focus of our early ancestors' lives was the physical reality and presence of the Nefilim and their role as our creators and their masters.

---

irony in the title of the novel), into the Zagros mountains area and we had to fend for ourselves. That was a second event that pushed us in the direction of self-determination.

But there are two main characteristics of human psychology of the remote times that contrast with our own. The first was that the central focus of our ancestors' lives was the physical reality and presence of the Nefilim and their role as our creators and their masters which we are now only re-discovering. That constituted their reality, their world view. It is a sociological difference rather than a neurological difference, to be sure, but it is also the reason why the early manifestation of our drive to self-determination had a somewhat more practical character in the remote past. The drive to self-determination manifested not so much as a reflexive self-analysis—**they lived in a known world and they knew what they were**—as an assertion of independence. A single striking example is the attempt by humans to build a rocket type vehicle, a *shem*, in an attempt to journey into space as the Nefilim did (popularly known as the Tower of Babel story). The discovery so disturbed the Nefilim ("Now, anything which they shall scheme to do shall no longer be impossible for them") that they deliberately forced a multiplicity of languages upon us to inhibit us.

The story of Gilgamesh is an excellent illustration of the second characteristic of our early psychology that contrasts with our current: their attitude toward immortality. Gilgamesh claimed, demanded, the immortality that the Nefilim possessed on the basis that his mother was a Nefilim "goddess," a "middle management" level Nefilim, (his father was a king but human). It furnishes clues to several important factors in the metamorphosis of our psychological component. It demonstrates quite clearly that there was full knowledge of our origins, the precise relationship of the human to the Nefilim, the rules of heritage and of inheritance that were so important a part of the Nefilm culture, the fact that an important ruler such as Gilgamesh was still totally at the whim of the Nefilim and had to go begging for what he sought, and that immortality could be bestowed upon a human if the Nefilim so wished. The concept of immortality is most important here. Although we tend, in our cultural context at this time, to think of immortality as a future scientific breakthrough or a religious concept, the ancients thought of it in practical, legal terms. The fascinating and critical element demonstrated here obviously is the **claim** to relative immortality:

When we map the accumulated artifactual evidence onto the ground of the archaeological context which we now recognize, the anthropological theory of today must change.

the '"Gilgamesh factor." It is central to the drive to self-determination, ultimately is the goal of that powerful drive we manifest.

When we map the accumulated artifactual evidence unto the ground of the archaeological context which we now recognize, the anthropological theory of today must change.

As a single example of how our thinking must readjust, consider the following. As I began writing this chapter an exhibit opened in the American Museum of Natural History in New York City called "Dark Caves, Bright Visions," the "largest show of late Ice Age material ever mounted in the United States." It raises many more questions than it answers when taken in the **traditional** context. Anthropologists and paleontologists, working against the actual trace finds, date our earlier, cruder form, Neanderthal to around 100,000 years ago and our more advanced form, Cro-Magnon, to around 50,000 years ago in south Africa. The fact that there was a "quantum leap in cultural evolution" (=mind evolution) already clearly recognizable and that technology as sophisticated as a flute 32,000 years ago and cave art of a highly developed and sensitive type around 30,000 years ago continues to lead to speculation on the part of even the trained scientist that has a ring of wildness about it. Guesses that some invention such as an improved blade stimulated a cultural impetus to biological improvement; longer life span (20 years!) allowing greater continuity of transfer of cultural knowledge, etc. This type of speculation is forced by the prevalent acceptance of a view of evolution as continuous rather than interrupted; it is invalidated when one recognizes that human mind had the potential from the beginning.

As far back as we can "see" even with the blinders of the current theory's mind-set, our Cro-Magnon ancestors outside the city-centers lived lives culturally indistinguishable from the peak levels of civilization of the American Indian. And it is incontrovertible that the only thing that distinguished the psychology and culture of the American Indian from the European explorers and settlers was the higher level of mechanical technology of the latter. And the term "mechanical" is used here for precision; the European settlers were not more advanced, indeed were, in many areas, decadent compared to the American Indian culture which they ruthlessly destroyed.

When we adjust our thinking to the extent that we recognize the

Our metamorphosis exhibits a continuity in time, a logic, a nobility and a directionality against which the conventional academic history of psychology takes on a new meaning and significance.

potential of the human mind operating almost from our 300,000 year beginning, that our bicameral genetic makeup allowed our advanced Nefilim genes to empower a drive to independence, the mind set of our early ancestors orbited around the physical presence and domination of the Nefilim, that their concept of immortality was physical, our metamorphosis exhibits a continuity in time, a logic, a nobility and a directionality against which the conventional academic history of psychology takes on a new meaning and significance.

For, unfortunately, if we turn to the academic world for insight and understanding of the nature and functioning of the human mind it seems as if we are short-changed; certainly there is a wealth of detailed knowledge concerning the operations of the mind available from accumulated research but, as with the subject of our real beginnings in general, the topic and definition of the human mind is dealt with in an attitude of stilted neutrality, bound by the splints of special interests.

The first thing that the student of the history of Psychology becomes aware of, on opening a typical standard text on the subject, is that, if one takes the presentation at face value, there is nothing to know about human psychology before the Greeks! The traditional pedagogical way of presenting the history of Psychology and the concepts of mind begins with the Greek philosophers who thought in terms of mind as soul, a unitary entity independent of the body and the highest form of which was *nous*, intelligence. Even the encyclopedia articles in our libraries today follow this format—parallel to the backwardness of Cambridge, only forty-five years ago, commencing history in Athens. If any excuse is offered for beginning at that point in time it is that the thought of the Greek philosophers supposedly marks the beginnings of what can be recognized as a science of psychology. Some scholars have even waxed rhapsodic enough to claim that the Greeks "discovered" mind, the logical and rational modes of thought. This traditional approach simply chooses to ignore the fact that the finest minds of the relatively recent and young Greek culture freely acknowledged the fact that they acquired almost everything from the much more ancient and mature cultures of Egypt and the Middle East. This is but one example of how our cultural mind-set conditions our perceptions. Even in as modern as work as Sidney Brett's *Psychology, Ancient and Modern* (1963), "ancient" means Greek, Aristotle and Plato and no reason is even suggested why the

We must recognize the strength of the Judaeo-Christian dye in the fabric of Western culture influencing the thinking of the modern academic thinkers.

Classical era should be the starting point. That Greek thought was already quite developed and robust, presupposing a source and considerable time for that development preceding them, is clear:

> Between 500 B.C. and A.D. 200 the ancient world presents a specimen of every known kind of psychological enquiry. The earliest stage furnishes scientific or objective accounts of perception and thought. From Socrates onward we find this supplemented by introspective and analytical work, with corollaries touching on immortality and kindred subjects. Aristotle carries this progress to its highest point in a mixed presentation of medical, biological, and philosophical doctrines. Even experiment is not wholly neglected, for the famous experiment of holding a marble between crossed fingers is ascribed to Aristotle. The spiritual or mystical vein is found in Plato and zealously worked by some of the later writers, especially by the Christian Platonists of Alexandria (c. A.D. 200)[19]

Little attention is given to the sources of Greek thought, the ancient Egyptian culture with its 700,000 volume library in Alexandria, the older cultures of the eastern Mediterranean and Middle East or the traditions stemming from as far back as Sumeria. What is recognized, usually with a great deal of diplomatic circumspection, is the moratorium that the coming to ascendancy of the moralistic doctrines of Christianity created in our general development. The point here is that we must recognize the strength of the Judaeo-Christian dye in the fabric of Western culture influencing the thinking of the modern academic thinkers to the extent that, not only do they not see the wealth of knowledge already accumulated before the Greek culture even appeared but they sometimes are not even aware of the influence of the Judaeo-Christian context within which they continue to think.

Tracing the academic approach further, one finds that, implicitly or explicitly acknowledging the one thousand year doldrums period in Western culture caused by the shift to the dogmatic domination of theological faith in the Christian Middle Ages, the traditional schema recognizes the resurgence of a freer and more humanistic concept of man and the human mind in the Renaissance, giving way to the more and more materialistic orientations of the Age of Reason, the growth of the

The most nocuous implication, however, is that the humans that preceded the Greeks were somehow of a lesser mental quality.

mechanistic concept of Man the Machine, the intelligent automaton. (One must still look outside the walls of academia to find the more recently developed concepts of mind as sophisticated bio-computer, and, lately, man and mind as reality creator.)

Giving due recognition to the fact that textbooks, by their nature, are out of date by the time they are published it remains true that the main deficiency with the textbooks of Psychology is that their authors are conditioned to judge what is truly significant psychology by comparison with western cultural standards. That is why the textbooks of Psychology, to be precise, deal with the pre-Cartesian era under the polite heading of the *philosophic* background of Psychology, implying that there is no psychology that does not use some sort of modern statistical, scientific approach. The most nocuous implication, however, is that the humans that preceded the Greeks were somehow of a lesser mental quality. That attitude is simply a manifestation of the same general attitude of western scholars examined in the previous chapter due to the fact that those peoples were pre-Christian, held to deal in myth and, therefore, to be inferior.

Although the traditional attitudes toward our nature and our mind are important enough to warrant a digression to evaluate, they no longer carry the weight and authority of previous times. We should simply appreciate the potential and utilize that perspective to enable us to proceed to construct the most intelligent future of which we are capable at this time.

The characteristics of our early mind set therefore can be summarized as relatively full-blown, capable of rapid assimilation of knowledge, seeking self-assertion yet conditioned by an absolute domination by the Nefilim. The mind-set and setting of subsequent times, however, begin to show a different character.

It was not until the end of the Egyptian dynasties that the shift from the assertion of independence and immortality as a legal right (if one was of the proper lineage) to the mode of self-analysis and self-determination begins to manifest as a function of the gradual weakening of the direct influence of the Nefilim. They first withdrew one step when they began appointing kings as overseers. They were influenced in their decisions by the often fierce contests for power and rulership among themselves and finally divided up the planet into regions, one of which was their exclusive domain

As the Nefilim presence gradually faded, vital ceremonies and rituals deteriorated or became corrupted, the high held in contempt.

and space port. They became less and less visible. Intermarriage with humans appears to be the cardinal cause of both the gradual recession, or diffusion, of Nefilim presence and dominance but also of the acceleration of the human metamorphic process. Although the cyclical spurts of progress and culture manifest in our history coincide with the probable return of their planet to the inner solar system, the time between those returns is lengthy in human terms (3600 years). As a result the contact with the Nefilim fades into a hazy and sometimes lost remembrance and understanding. That is why human understanding of our genesis and remote history has reached its present state. It is also the reason we can trace a gradual transition between the time of practical assertion of independence and the almost obsessive seeking of self-understanding. Succeeding generations experiencing the genetic imperative drive of the advanced Nefilim genes, manifest the collective characteristics of a questing to discover who and what they were.

The Egyptians, to cite a single example of the transitional phase, had direct contact with the Nefilim at the beginning of their very lengthy history and civilization. They knew them as physically present, knew their rulers, worked under the direction of and with their lower echelon technicians. They knew their rules of conduct and inheritance, knew as demi-gods those who were of both Nefilim and human parentage, knew their role in that highly structured, hierarchical society. As the Nefilim presence gradually faded, vital ceremonies and rituals deteriorated or became corrupted, the high held in contempt. It is worth noting here that immortality was a given for the Nefilim but could have become more and more uncertain as cross breeding with human stock progressed. It is entirely **speculative** at this point but the reason for the gradually increasing fragility of the physical nature of the Egyptian rulers may have been due to that intermixing and the elaborate preservation of the remains of the rulers with an obvious orientation to immortality was a way of preserving the essential cellular structure so that, on periodic return of the Nefilim, advanced techniques of cloning or restoration could be exercised. Disturbing of the ancient tombs and scattering of remains worldwide may be a far more serious matter than we previously have considered it. The viewing of a team of specialists attempting to remove some tissue residue from a mummy in an attempt to obtain genetic material for analysis (TV documentary) recently was a bit

> **Put it in whatever terms you wish: the "robot" has been working, continually, even obsessively, to discover its own nature.**

eerie. By our time even the Egyptians seem to have forgotten the real past—or perhaps it is the voices of the Western scholars, puzzling over the ruins and the archaeological traces, that we hear and mistakenly accept as the voice of that ancient culture.

Once we have adjusted our view and understanding of ourselves in the past, the patterns of the present take on a deeper meaning. When we step back and look retrospectively over the entire history of human culture and especially the psychological component in particular there is an unmistakable pattern of development, an overriding, preoccupying theme clear to our view: the preoccupation of the human race has been with the process of self-discovery both physically and mentally.

All of the various disciplines have ultimately been used to contribute to the deeper and more precise knowledge of the human condition and the human being on all levels; the fundamental philosophical questions Who are we? What are we? What is our purpose? How do we function? are the real questions always just under the surface of our seeking self-improvement.

Put it in whatever terms you wish: the "robot" has been working, continually, even obsessively, to discover its own nature. It is essential to note that the **"robot"** concept is *metaphorical*. It is also very appropriate in that the Nefilim intended us to be just a bit above that level and for purposes with which we, currently, usually associate robots. We even play with thinking of ourselves in such terms and our science fiction is filled with variations on that theme. By comparison with the level of consciousness toward which we all know we are gradually evolving as a species our consciousness may seem "robot." Nietzsche said in Thus Spake Zarathurstra What is man? A bridge between the ape and superman—a bridge over an abyss. He would perhaps have been pleased at the resolution of his vision.

The drive to self-realization, individually and racially, has five positive and one negative components all of which are essentially mental/psychological.

1. **Self-determination**: the more specific the understanding and control the "robot" has gained over itself the greater is the drive to self-definition and autonomy: our collective psychology.

Immortality becomes more of a recognizable and desirable goal and emerges as a primary characteristic of the next plateau of human metamorphosis.

---

2. **Philosophical relativism**: as the knowledge gained from self-inspection has led to a more and more acute understanding of the subjective relativism of our perception we have developed a highly solipsistic epistemology and relativistic explanation of "reality": our philosophy.

3. **Seeking a common bonding**: the greater and greater realization of the generic characteristics of human nature conbined with a deeper sense of subjective relativism tends to drive us to seek a generic common bond.

4. **Redefinition of transcendence**: as the subjective neurological nature of our experience has become more obvious and manipulable it has led to a gradual re-definition of religious or transcendental experience in terms of neurological expansion: our religion.

5. **Preoccupation with immortality**: as self-determination increases the possibility of relative physical immortality becomes more of a recognizable and desirable goal and emerges as a primary characteristic of the next plateau of human metamorphosis.

6. **Reactive Suppression**: to the degree the "robot" seeks autonomy and independence so do the established "robot" political, religious, military and social institutions exert greater and greater power to control the "robots," to maintain the *status quo*: our sociological history.

In *The Five Ages of Man*,[20] Gerald Heard outlined the sweeping panorama of that human quest. Working against the postulate that ontogeny follows phylogeny (the development of an human individual recapitulates rapidly, from conception to death, the stages of evolution through which the race has already passed), he gives meaning to the broad patterns of our known historical behavior. He identified several general phases: tribal consciousness; the hero; the ascetic; the domestic; the post domestic.

1. Tribal consciousness: the type of consciousness in which the individual is aware of self predominantly as a member of a group. Associated with controlled rites of initiation (ritualized stress) as well as the shamanistic practices of inducing visionary experience. (Parallel birth to a few years.)

The obsessive drive to self-discovery is the primary manifestation of the rapid metamorphosis which we are collectively experiencing.

2. The transition stage of the hero, the over-corrective affirmation of individuality—sometimes at almost any cost—incorporated alcohol as its specific drug of ritualized preparation for or release from the awful pressures of conflict, combat, conquest and defeat (parallel the ages of 9 to 12—the age of GI-Joe, Superman).

3. The age of asceticism (monasticism is seen as a world-wide phenomenon in this context), the rejection of the heroic ego, using systematic sensory deprivation, fasting, sleep deprivation, etc. to change and expand consciousness (parallel the age of puberty and caffeine as its specific drug).

4. The stage of first maturity, the responsible parent in the domesticated, family context.

5. The stage of second maturity, the individual free to retire from the responsibility of parentage and explore the areas of higher consciousness.

Although Heard did not have the critical advantage of the archaeological perspective we now possess, his work still made patent the rapidity, the vast changes, and the precocity of the human drama. He provided a framework much larger and more accurate than the traditional academic treatment and taught us that, to identify the beginnings of our knowledge and definition of mind in the remote past we must turn to the paleontologist and the archaeologist rather than the academic psychologist or the historian.

It is clear that the obsessive drive to self discovery is the primary manifestation of the rapid metamorphosis which we are collectively experiencing. It can best be understood as a kind of genetic imperative engendered by our bicameral makeup. The "robot," at a more and more accelerated pace, openly and freely in an open and free society or secretly in a repressive society, will manipulate itself, experiment, test itself, pry into its circuitry, map its components, understand its own design and maintenance, use that information to improve the present and create its own future.

Individuals of Homo-Erectus-Nefilimus, depending on their particular genetic programming, will sometimes blow a few "circuits" trying

The techniques we have used to pry into our circuitry, expand our modes of consciousness to new frequencies of energy, are culturally varied and numerous.

or even die in the attempt. There is a Taoist legend concerning the last words of a monk. In a time when his peers were preoccupied with determining the physiological/mental altering properties of every substance they could ingest, he was heard to say just before he fell, dead, from eating the bark of the very top of a certain tree, "Not that oneeeee!" All humans, when they allow themselves to be in their most natural state, empathize with the motif and black humor of that story.

The techniques we have used to pry into our circuitry, become directly conscious of unconscious-autonomic processes, reflexively experience ourselves experiencing, expand our modes of consciousness to new frequencies of energy, are culturally varied and numerous.

Although not everyone is knowledgeable about the various types of yogas practiced for centuries in the East, we are all familiar with the general concept of yoga as a technique to gain control over autonomic functions, achieve mind control, open the consciousness to more subtle forms of energy and information. We have all been made aware, if only by the documentaries viewed through television, of the various rituals and ceremonies, drugs and disciplines used the world over to alter, improve, control, manipulate, expand human awareness. It is common knowledge that shamans the world over, from the American Indians, to Central Americn natives, to the Greek oracle temples to the banks of the Ganges systematically altered and studied consciousness, found wisdom and practical knowledge through stress inducing ceremonies, psychosomatic induction by the use of chanting and sound, confinement in darkness, specifically selected chemical extracts of plants. Fewer are aware of the archaeological finds in the far northern Siberian wastes of hemp, cannabis, showing that it was known and being smoked or ingested by the prehistoric Ice Age peoples many thousands of years ago. Fewer are aware that the Christian monks of the deserts of Egypt, epitomized by Anthony or Jerome, systematically used fasting (the beginnings of Lenten practices in Christendom) and exposure to the extremes of the desert clime and celibacy as techniques to expand their consciousness in their quest for experience of the transcendent. Mostly scholars are aware that alcohol, opium, absynthe, strong coffee, nicotine were appreciated in most of Europe not too long ago in a different way than that in which the American government wishes its people to view them now and that Freud used cocaine as an exploratory tool.

We are at a pivotal point of momentous significance in our history; we now understand the nature of the obsessive drive to self-discovery, the reason for it and the ramifications of that knowledge for the future.

But no one can miss the widespread preoccupation with consciousness change both positive and negative that modern man is involved in at present. Consciousness now can be manipulated chemically through the entire spectrum from coma to ecstasy, for good or ill, for expansion or contraction, for enrichment, wisdom or self-destruction, the benefit or control and destructions of others, for transcendence or reduction to the vegetative state. To condemn all use as abuse and to attempt to wipe out an activity that, in historical and psychological perspective, is so fundamental to the human quest is to ignore the neuro-chemical nature of consciousness, hopeless and absurd. History has shown quite clearly that legally or illegally, overtly or covertly, as part of the dominant culture or the counter-culture we will pry into our circuitry, learn our systems. There has been and will be no preventing the "robot" from self-discovery.

The past has seen us dance, whirl, fast, meditate, pray non-stop, practice celibacy and ritual sex, chant, go without sleep, use magic, mudras, mantras, yogas of all types, pain, as well as immersion, sensory deprivation and drugs. Because our present technology is focused on the molecular level of reality, the robot's consciousness and self-exploration is preoccupied with molecular tools, ie. drugs; "better living through chemistry," to borrow from a large chemical corporation. Electronics will furnish us other new tools as will almost unimaginable technologies in the future. The robot, historically, has used and will use whatever tool is available.

Although the process of self-discovery is almost intuitively apparent to everyone, our perception of it has been simply as an ongoing, hopefully up-levelling process, sometimes puzzling, sometimes exhilarating, sometimes fraught with risk. **But we are at a pivotal point of momentous significance in our history; we now understand the nature of the obsessive drive to self-discovery, the reason for it and the ramifications of that knowledge for the future.**

The most cogent reason appears to lie in the nature of our genetic creation in the past, the combination of a relatively primitive set of genes

The quest for self-understanding, self-determination is the central, positive, essential focus of human nature to which we should devote high energy and intelligence.

and an advanced set which act as a driving force behind the process. The history of the process is the manifestation of our resultant, rapid positive metamorphic development as a mutant species.

The key is to see the quest for what it is, understand the mechanisms that are involved and intelligently and consciously educate concerning them as part of our common planetary cultural heritage. The quality of our future depends on how well and how rapidly we assimilate that knowledge and intelligently utilize it. When we allow ourselves to treat ourselves in the past in the persepctive of our true genesis and metamorphosis we find keys to the real significance of many models and phases of our accumulated psychological knowledge and, ultimately, our concept of mind. Once we have seen the pattern the details of its elements become clear. To say it in a slightly more technical but precise way, recognition of the genetic imperative impulse behind the metamorphic nature of the robot's quest immediately throws its component psychological vectors sharply into focus. We should now recognize that the quest for self-understanding, self-determination is the central, positive, essential focus of human nature to which we should devote high energy and intelligence. We should be aware of the contribution to the collective human situation its pursuit brings. The value of the right to pursue it should be acknowledged and carefully guarded.

The sometimes dry and often tedious narrations of the history of Psychology, in terms of who-did-what-when, we find in textbooks or Encyclopedias suddenly comes alive against this background. The linear trend over time shows a clearly defined intensification from Locke and Berkeley through Hume, Muller, von Hemholtz, Fechner, Wundt, Ebbinghaus, Tichener, James, Dewey, Watson, Werthheimer, etc. of the attempt to gain more and more minute information about mechanisms, how the robot functioned. With Freud, Jung, Adler we see the "repair mechanics" using verbal and other probes in attempts to diagnose and correct defects in the robot.

Jung's archetypes and concept of the collective unconscious is better understood in terms of a bicameral mind and a bicameral genetic racial heritage.

The most critical element in human psychology that we must deal with is imprinting.

The concept of therapeutic treatment for conflicts is better understood against the background of a genetic heritage which may have inherent tendencies to cause them if the genetic engineering that produced us was halted at the point of a satisfactory product relative to the needs of the Nefilim. They may have not been any more concerned with product life and performance than we are when we use a chimpanzee as a first test subject in manned rocketry. It is purely speculative at this point to suggest that the widespread mental illness and literally thousands of genetically based diseases we have seen characteristically in the human race may be the result of the arbitrary aims and standards of the Nefilim in the process of our invention but it is certainly a subject that demands investigation. The importance of the subject will spur the development of the ingenious genetic techniques required.

Gerald Heard broke ground in approaching history from the psychological-sociological perspective rather than the "drum and trumpet" mode that tends to record the martial convulsions of the body politic in the extremes of war, revolutions, conquest and defeat. If he provided us with an initial framework, within the old context of a linear evolution, of the history of the working out of the effect of the metamorphic vectors in the past, it is Timothy Leary who has provided the refined model, in his *Info-Psychology* (New Falcon Publications, 1993), for the understanding of how those vectors have manifested in the present and appear to be going to manifest in the future.

Leary characterizes the human neurological system in terms of "circuits" that turn on sequentially from the time of birth to maturity. He identifies four planet-oriented, "larval," survival circuits: bio-survival, emotional-locomotion, laryngeal-manual dexterity, sexual-domestication and four "future" oriented circuits: neuro-somatic, neuro-electric, neurogenetic, metaphysiological-neuro-atomic. His position is that the most critical element in human psychology that we must deal with is **imprinting,** the physio-psychological process that absorbs a neurological "photograph" that is embedded, usually permanently, at critical points of an individual's development and which "determines the positive and negative foci for subsequent conditioning of the newly activated neural circuit." He recognizes and sums up elegantly the nature of the historical drive for self-exploration and self-realization

Rudimentary recognition of the larval, cyclical nature of contemporary

Leary is already speaking in terms of the metamorphosis of larval humanity.

human existence has been sporadically attained in earlier civilizations which have temporarily reached the necessary level of biological, political, technological, and reproductive security. In ancient China, India, Ceylon, Crete, Babylon, Greece, Islamic Damascus, Egypt, Renaissance Europe, a few neurologically elite, premature evolutes have used aesthetic expressions, science-fiction speculations and botanical methods of expanding neurological function beyond survival imprints.[21]

Although he also works against a linear evolution, his clinically precise identification of the "future" circuits is invaluable.

The Neurosomatic Circuit—mediating the reception, integration and transmission of sensory-somatic signals un-censored by larval imprints and designed to operate in zero-gravity environment. Body consciousness.

The Neuro-Electric Circuit which receives, integrates and transmits neural signals from all the other circuits and from the brain at the simultaneity and velocity of a bio-electric grid; not programmed by survival imprints. Brain consciousness.

The neurogenetic Circuit imprints the DNA code, receiving, integrating and transmitting RNA signals, thus operating at species-time, making possible biological immortality, and symbiosis with Higher Life forms. DNA consciousness.

The Metaphysiological-Neuro-Atomic Circuit is activated when the nervous system imprints sub-nuclear quantum-mechanical and gravitational signals, thus transcending biological existence. Quantum consciousness.[21]

Leary is already speaking in terms of the **metamorphosis** of larval humanity (the first four bio-survival circuits) into post-terrestrial humanity (the four future circuits as above) the process being under the direction of our genetic code. We need only map his elegant advanced model on the ground of the expanded archaeological perspective to integrate past, present and future. Leary's primary interest as a psychologist in the specific chemical compounds called psychedelics is based on his recognition that they are the only type of substances yet known (heavy trauma, childbirth, near-death experiences can also but they certainly are not convenient means) that reach down far enough into the neurological system to actually allow effective

The futant is now clinically identifiable as a positive genetic type.

change of behavior under the control of the individual by allowing re-imprinting. If we think of the four future circuits he delineates as the manifestation of the potential of our advanced Nefilim genetic components so much falls immediately into place. What Leary and other psychedelic explorers have discovered experientially and empirically is immanently logical relative to both what history indicates we might expect and the reasons we have advanced here for our obsessive self-analysis. Although we could have just as well evolved in other directions it is clear that, as a race, our focus is spaceward. Again, the correlation is obvious. The Nefilim were skilled space travellers, they came from "out there"; perfection, heaven, godliness, the goal is "up there." We take the idea that "heaven" is "up" so much for granted because of that ancient orientation embedded in our collective consciousness. Any suggestion that goes contrary to the sublimated concept of a blissful afterlife being in "heaven" or the heavens seems akin, to many, to denying a law of physics. We are so close to the association of the concepts of heaven and immortality that it is difficult for some to wake up enough to take a second look at that ancient concept as the amalgam of the two characteristics possessed by the Nefilim that humans were not granted: the ability to travel in the heavens to and from their home planet and their relative immortality.

As part of his model Leary also identifies a genetic type for which he has coined a word: a "futant," one whose future circuits have begun to be activated, whose genetic direction is to explore the future. His position is that all humans can and should open up these circuits that mark the path of our future metamorphosis/evolution. **The futant is now clinically identifiable as a positive genetic type**, a small, perhaps 2 to 3 percent, part of the population. There is also a pattern discernible in our racial history that allows us to identify a specialized group of futants, extant at any given time within the population, naturally selected to facilitate the survival of the species by actively exploring future possibles and, incidentally, taking the brunt of the risk better through specifically adapted genetic characteristics. Every culture and time has seen them. Some cultures have recognized and respected and utilized their abilities. Some have ostracized, or imprisoned and even killed them. The Brunos, the Galileos, the Le Maitres, etc.

Perhaps, through a combination of the impress of the growing

**If one person has reached a certain stage of metamorphosis/
evolution, the entire race has attained it.**

orientation to the future, the acceleration of our space ventures, the
immediacy of the unknown, the weakening and atrophying of the
traditional religions we have begun to recognize the role of the futant-
pioneer again. Mapped on the background of our unique genesis we see that
the futant type, although neither different or superior, has a particular role
at the forefront of our metamorphosis. And who are they? Those of us who
are programmed to be the scouts in front of the wagon-train, handicapped,
perhaps, in so far as we probably could not do otherwise, ready to risk the
arrow or the micrometeorite for knowledge of what's up ahead, who are
programmed to the future rather than the past, who live in the future in so
far as what seems remote to many is already obvious and present to them.
The critical realization, in view of our quest for self-knowledge and self-
determination and control of our own evolution, is that we must recognize
the futant type for what they are and take advantage of their talent. To
disregard that valuable resource is a tragic waste. Once we have recognized
the nature of the drive to self-exploration and its relationship to our future
metamorphosis it should be easier to integrate the function of the futant
into the human context. The expression of the advanced genetic components
may even be surprising for the futant. Unless we recognize and provide a
positive context of freedom in which the futant type is recognized and can
operate and in which the dross can be separated from valuable information
we will be depriving the race of a vital contribution.

If one person has reached a certain stage of metamorphosis/evolution, the
entire race has attained it.

The most important realization of the 90s will be the direct connection of
our unique genesis with the nature of the leading edge of our metamorphic
psychology. When we have recognized that continuity, all of the history of
our psychological research and exploration becomes more meaningful and
intelligible. Having gained that perspective, it will serve us well to re-survey
and re-interpret the history of our psychological quest. It seems clear as well
as reaching a level of technological development to understand the scientific
concepts involved in our genesis (genetic engineering), we had to develop to
a level of psychological maturity to allow ourselves to see the situation as it
really is, to become self-confident enough to accept it. The race, in the
overall perspective, has just reached the end of its adolescence and is
beginning the classic **separation** from its parents. Having established its

If we truly have exhibited "robot" characteristics we may now see that syndrome for what it is: a manifestation of the peaking of our obsessive self-analysis which has produced a transcendent result.

---

basic independence perhaps a recognition and reconciliation may take place. Several important factors may influence the events of the near future in what may be seen as a generation of transition.

The dark side clearly will be the part of robot mentality that, frozen in the sublimated obsequious posture of the master-slave relationship, will object most to the concepts put forth here, that most fears "the godlike in ourselves." It will be this mentality that, once the facts can no longer be denied, will make a faith-religion out of a revived worship (the original meaning of the word was **"work"**) of the Nefilim, and a cargo-cult temple out of Arecibo. Sad, but seemingly inevitable: the "we are not our own master" syndrome, a negative component vector in the metamorphosis of our psychology.

Those who can achieve an adult perspective will welcome the passing of the mysteries of our genesis, and having learned the racial "facts of life," will go on to mine the past and re-interpret the present to create the future.

The ramifications for the discipline of Psychology as such are clear.

In one stroke the entire western religio-cultural barrier that prevents us from penetrating the real psychology of human nature prior to the Greeks is eliminated.

One has only to reflect a little to recognize what reams of material will result in Jungian circles from the concept that our bicameral heritage endows us with an amalgam of **two** racial genetic memory data-banks, a bicameral collective unconscious.

A new context for the study of our genetic coding opens up. Do we see psychological throwbacks to Homo-Erectus elements in some forms of our retardations? Can we account for the redundancies and "nonsense" coding, possible histone masking, genetic disease, insanity, by analyzing for logical clues to imperfect engineering of our beginnings?

But the two major critical results of our new perception surpass the academic re-interpretations and readjustments by many magnitudes.

The most immediate result will be that we now have the keys to break not only the interminable dreary recycling of academic pomposities about what we are but also to replace the "robot" metaphor introduced into the common consciousness by the brilliant LeMaitre in *L'Homme Machine*

There is a condition that is both essential to and a product of philotropic humanism: immortality

(Man the Machine) in the 18th century. If we truly have exhibited "robot" characteristics and spoken of ourselves in that way, we may now see that syndrome for what it is: a manifestation of the peaking of our obsessive self-analysis, the pressure and intensity of which has culminated in a degree of self-awareness that has actually produced a transcendent result. We should remind ourselves, however, that, in the light of the very re-discovery that we have made, it will inevitably be a temporary plateau. We obviously have not finished mapping ourselves as "robot"; the developments in neurophysics, molecular/atomic biology soon to be abetted by the new STM (scanning tunnelling microscopes), psychopharmacology, Kirlian photography, etc. attest to that. There will be negative social pressures and a constant, nagging, uneasy inertial influence from the unintegrated, undigested belief systems of the scientists themselves. But there will eventually be no containing the elational freedom of a race which is its own master, knowing a generic common bond stronger than outmoded separatist doctrines in a common genesis. The mapping of the "robot" will no longer tend to be confined to certain neutral areas to avoid the taboos of "philosophy, politics and religion," will progress at an even more accelerated rate—yet give way to and become subsumed into a consciously exercised philtropic (generic wisdom seeking) humanism. Only this level of vision can generate the positive optimism that is necessary for its own implementation.

But there is a condition that is both essential to and a product of philotropic humanism: immortality. We are no longer—have really never been—obligated by our primitive belief systems to capitulate to an ancient outmoded mechanism inherited from assimilated lower plant and animal forms that may have been a valid evolutionary survival gambit for them: cyclical sacrificial fertilization to rapidly build up an organic layer for propagation of their phylums on a rocky planet. The attainment of relative immortality will be the next turning point in our racial history. Under whatever guise, in whatever context, religious, philosophical, occult, mystical or scientific, we have been seeking that which, because of the ancient taboos, we fear the most, "the god-like in ourselves," the chief distinguishing characteristic that the Nefilim possessed and would not give to us. Immortality is the goal of self-awareness, self-consciousness, self-knowledge, self-determination. Not primarily the "good life," not "harmony

Ultimately, immortality is a matter of simple human dignity.

---

with others," not "enlightenment," not "life **after** death": **immortality in space-time.** When we are totally honest with ourselves. That is the reason why we have clung to the doctrines that say the "soul is immortal." That is why we have endured the hollow symbols and rituals of primitive religious systems on the basis of an act of faith to this point in time. The deep genetic conviction that somehow there may be a key buried in those doctrines and practices that even the unlettered are cynical about . . . Relative immortality is a matter of practical expediency; we need the time for the individual to acquire the wisdom, the knowledge, that experience that fulfills the human potential—and will make us cosmic citizens. We may not qualify unless we do. There have been a number of books written on the subject since the 1970s; scientists are expending a great deal of energy on many phases of research in that area; the concept has rapidly become a part of the common consciousness. Ultimately relative immortality is a matter of simple human dignity. And the vectors, after converging at the point of the new "immortal" human, will just as sharply diverge as we begin to freely expand into the age of real self-determination. The psychology of immortality remains to be written.

It is the nature of this new humanism which we will develop in the following chapters as we trace the many separate vectors of current and perennial thought converging in our time on that focus of vision.

CHAPTER 6
BUT HOW DO WE KNOW IT'S TRUE?

We need to take control of the context of our lives. It's in the context that we find the meaning.

Gene Youngblood

The reader deserves an explanation, at this point, of the mind-set of the author regarding the criteria by which the interpretation of the archaeological and historical information, accumulated over the last century, and the speculative philosophizing presented here for which it is a key catalyst, can be shown to be valid, to be true and accurate. The demand for proof is singularly justified and cogent not only because it is a vitally consequential subject but also because one of the primary inescapable ramifications of the general thesis requires us to radically reevaluate the historical events and the institutions that gave rise to the very criteria which are consensually used to evaluate the proof!

It should be recognized that the requirement of substantial proof of the ideas advanced here would not be necessary if our cultural heritage was unbroken from the beginning. If there was a continuous linear development there might be disagreement, over time, concerning the minutiae of details or dates or the spelling of names or arcane disputes about individual evens or the intentions of characters but not about the fundamental facts about the foundations of our planetary history. But our various cultural histories have not evolved as structures built on the ancient, immovable foundations. They are far more like the naive structures built by children mimicking the actions of adults, constructed from mental concepts only partly understood, based on no solid foundation. This is true, perhaps, to a far greater degree in the West than in the East.

In the East the connection with the ancient root-culture and history, although somewhat corrupted through separation in time, and sometimes hardened into a shallow pietism, is far more intact. An example that dearly illustrates the contrast between the Western and Eastern mind-sets is drawn from a recent television program on modern India. A woman, widowed, and apparently in her late thirties, had become a

In contemporary Western culture we identify three major criteria bases: philosophical, scientific and theological, in alphabetical order in the name of impartiality.

professional architect and was the focal point of a section of the program. She had gained great respect, understandably from the examples presented throughout the documentary, for her work in buildings and renovations which blended a modern approach with motifs, techniques, materials and themes from the ancient traditions in building and design of her country's culture and tradition. She obviously was a person of artistic sensitivity as well as modern technical ability and knowledge. Yet she was able to state, quite simply and factually, while displaying the intricately woven and remarkable fabrics produced by a family in the country, that this same family had been producing these special and very specific patterns and materials unchanged for some five thousand years and that they had originally been produced "for the gods." Literally.

In the West the militant attitude of the Jewish religious culture regarding paying attention to "other gods" springing from the dictatorial mandates of Yahweh the Nefilim patron of the Jewish tribe—"you shall have no other gods before me"—reinforced the divisions already existing as a result of the imposed divisiveness by multiplicity of language. Yahweh was a "jealous god" because he did not want his human subjects to work for (the original meaning of the word worship) or give allegiance to his kin in other territories. Those strictures were transmitted through to Western culture when Christianity transmuted them into social laws and was enabled, for a considerable period, to systematically and ruthlessly stamp out any and all references to the common ancient root culture that recognized the Nefilim, the "gods.""Pagan," that deeply embedded term which has its root meaning in the concept of "country dweller" but signifies the worst of polytheism in the Christian tradition, that term of anathema, has contributed critically in a tremendously greater measure to the erection of the ideological barrier that prevents us from intelligently evaluating and incorporating the vast ancient common root history of our race than the critical mind-set of the Greeks. Even the most skeptical of the Greeks, who rejected obviously naive explanations of the formation of the earth, the nature of natural phenomena as myth and even criticized popular religions had no barrier against examining that ancient tradition and evaluating it.

In contemporary Western culture we identify three major criteria bases: philosophical, scientific and theological, in alphabetic order in the name of impartiality.

When the same individual is a theologian, a philosopher and a scientist the problems of conflicting criteria can become acute. Consider the classic case of the Jesuit, Teilhard de Chardin.

The philosopher/rationalist puts his faith in the primary efficacy of the logical process to determine the validity of the conclusions drawn from the information available.

The scientist depends on the empirical process and statistical analysis to validate or invalidate the hypotheses under investigation.

The theologian and the believer look to faith, an act of assent to ideas which cannot be proven as true, except on the basis of an appeal to the authority of a Higher Power, for the verification of the truth of lesser information.

These categories, introduced for clarity and definition, can be seen, by even the reader who has never had occasion to deeply consider the subject before, to be oversimplified. A single example of the crossover complexity in the real world is the occultist. A current tendency in the work of philosophers who are open enough to examine the occult from a scientific point of view is to apply the epistemology of a different type of consciousness as a means of truth-test. Synchronicity, if looked on scientifically, would be considered a relative philosophical criteria; if there was a connection attributed to a Higher Power or divinity of some sort it could qualify as theological. In any individual they merge, blend, overlap, cause tension, are used alternately, randomly and sometimes simultaneously. The theologian will appeal to reason to show you the rationality of faith as a criteria of truth; the rationalist puts his faith in reason to judge the religious exercise of faith or the empirical method as a criteria; the empiricist will reason with you to show you that reason and logic or faith do not approach the effectiveness of the empirical method in which he or she has put faith.

When the same individual is a theologian, a philosopher and a scientist the problems of conflicting criteria can become acute. Consider the classic case of the Jesuit, Teilhard de Chardin.

De Chardin was a devout Catholic believer and a trained theologian. As such, he would, or be required to, subject any facts under consideration to the criteria of those teachings which he held as unquestionably true because they had been revealed or dictated by an Authority of a higher order who is understood to be Ultimate Truth Itself. As a trained theologian, de Chardin operated in this manner in his role as a Catholic priest. The nature of reality,

To understand de Chardin's situation is to understand the problems of criteria in the modern West.

in this context, is arrived at by deductive reasoning; what is not immediately revealed is deduced by working from the general, revealed doctrines, to the particular consequences of those doctrines. Reason is used in this process as a tool but the conclusions must be in keeping with the revealed general principles or discarded. The basis of the entire process is an act of acceptance, assent, faith in the impeccability or infallibility of the source from which the revelation was received.

De Chardin was also a trained philosopher. The philosopher, traditionally using the reasoning process as a primary tool, works in an inductive manner, reasoning from the particular phenomena and facts that he observes and/or accepts to more and more general principles with the objective of arriving at the most fundamental, universal principles, ie. the ultimate nature of reality. Reason is again the tool but the criteria is not a received set of postulates, assumptions, but the laws of logic.

And de Chardin was also a scientist. As a paleontologist he was involved in the discovery of Peking Man. The scientist uses, as a fundamental tool, the empirical, observational method to determine the nature of either a particular part of reality or to work toward the discovery of the more and more universal laws that govern reality. (Paleontology is not as precise a science as quantum physics but is certainly rigorous in its evaluation of the observed evidence and facts through the use of advanced techniques for dating, chemical analysis, and geological stratigraphy.)

To understand the conflicts which de Chardin experienced one must understand the development of the relationship between theology, philosophy and science as it has evolved in Western culture. To understand de Chardin's situation is to understand the problems of criteria in the modern West.

Historically, philosophy (philo-sophia, love of wisdom in the Greek), originally encompassed all of human knowledge including theology, the sciences, arts and mathematics. Due to the ascendance of Catholicism in Western culture asserting the divine authority of the Bible and the doctrine of infallibility of the Pope of Rome, theology gradually attained a separate status and tended to dominate all other disciplines. Witness the Inquisition.

The differences and the conflicts between the three disciplines has

For every criterion of truth and reality one selects, one can ask the question: by what criterion do I judge that the criterion which I have selected is correct?

obviously been the result of the differences between the criteria used by each one. It is also true that, historically, the development of the scientific method came about, partially, as a result of a reaction to the deductive orientation of the theologian. In the extreme case, the scientist who, using rigorous and meticulous methods, arrives at a conclusion about a certain facet of reality, obviously finds it difficult to reject his conclusive findings because the religious system to which he happens to adhere informs him that it is not in keeping with its doctrine. Witness Galileo. De Chardin, as a paleontologist, found himself in this position with regard to the evolutionary information confronting him as a result of his discovery of Peking man. He also came into conflict with, and was subsequently silenced by, the Church because of his erudite reasoning as a philosopher in articulating an evolutionary theory of the development of consciousness based on the evidence he possessed as a scientist, in spite of the fact that he envisioned, as a theologian, the culmination, the Omega point as he called it, of that evolution, as a fusion with the Divine principle, God, in the traditional Catholic sense. The general problems of criteria conflict are classically illustrated in the plight of de Chardin.

The general form of the problem may be defined even more accurately by the question What criterion does one use to determine what criterion to use? which puts one at the center of the philosophic debates which have raged now for centuries. At the present time there are far more radically diverging criteria than answers.

Those professionally familiar with the subject are well aware that, in the ongoing search for the ultimate criterion of truth and reality, Descartes turned thinking back on itself, Godel turned mathematics back on itself, G. Spencer Brown turned logic back on itself, Douglas Hofstader has turned solipsism back on itself and we still do not have a consensus except, perhaps, concerning the fact that we do not agree. The solipsism is of such an acute degree that we find the Phenomenologists telling us and each other that the most objective reality is that we cannot know objective reality so just forget trying. It has become the rage in some more sophisticated new age circles to fall back on a sort of Western Zen approach to the problem and say that, in effect, if we can't punch our way out of the epistemological paper bag then we should recognize the significance of that factual illusion as a key to the nature of the forest of trees from which the paper was made . . . If we cannot

Establishing a consensual criterion by which to judge if the archaeological information and the concepts put forth in this work are correct quite obviously presents a very unique challenge.

agree on a criterion, there is at least better agreement on the nature of the problem: for every criterion of truth and reality one selects, one can ask the question By what criterion do I judge that the criterion which I have selected is correct? The Achilles' heel of all argument based on reason is that one may continue to ask the same question as to what criterion of truth has been used to judge the veracity of whatever criterion is advanced. Who judges the judge who judges the judge who judges the judge etc. *ad infinitum*. At some point someone usually throws up their hands in exasperation and says "Well, you have to start some place!" Even that statement, I respectfully submit, is open to the same inevitable question (just, obviously, as is this statement itself). Another typical alternate reaction, somewhat more fashionable currently, is to say that, in the last analysis, it is all just subjective judgement based on subjective perception of the evidence. Again that position is open to the question By what criterion do you hold that true? An endless solipsistic loop.

While the philosophers and theologians argue and discuss the scientist is working on rigorously controlled duplicable experiments to prove, according to the empirical/statistical criterion if her or his theories are correct, often exhibiting little patience with the philosophical approach. Tell you the nature of the paper bag down to the quantum level? Sure thing. Criterion of truth? Not my department. The limitation of the scientific method is that there are some things and types of problems that are not manageable with its techniques.

The believer and the theologian who teaches believers wish to be reasonable but, when the chips are down, will simply fall back on doctrines that are accepted as revealed or unquestioned dogma. The empirical method and logic may be listened to but held as subservient to doctrines of faith.

Establishing a consensual criterion by which to judge if the archaeological information and the concepts put forth in this work are correct quite obviously presents a very unique challenge.

It is immediately apparent that the empirical method of rigorously repeatable experiment can only be applied in the very limited sense of checking the accuracy of carbon dating techniques or similar ancillary processes. Some wag has said that the only rigor in the science of

The validity of the Judaeo-Christian theological criterion itself is in question.

---

archaeology is in the digging. That certainly is a somewhat jaded witticism but it does point up the fact that one cannot do a dig over again, repeat an historical event, or apply statistical techniques in a meaningful way.

The difficulties are compounded by several magnitudes when we consider the position of the believer and the theologian. The unvarnished fact is that the acceptance of the thesis of this book involves recognition that the Divine Being, invoked as guarantor of the criterion of the believer and the theologian, is a concept developed from the relationship of the Hebrew people to their Nefilim ruler; Yahweh was a humanoid. The monotheism of the Old Testament which forms the bedrock principle of the Judaeo-Christian religions is clearly a sublimated form of the original pact between the Nefilim ruler of the district in which the original proto-Jews found themselves in trouble in the out-back when they agreed to keep his rules and serve him in return for his patronage and protection. No amount of torturous interpretation of Genesis can erase the repeated references to "the gods," the "sons of the gods," the Nefilim in view of the overwhelming documentation from the far more ancient and extensive Sumerian, Akkadian, Egyptian and other records. The validity of the Judaeo-Christian theological criterion itself is in question. The recovered information also shows that the "gods" spoken of in the Hindu and Eastern traditions as divine—although that term does not mean exactly the same as it does in Western culture—were the same Nefilim. Theological criteria are in trouble.

It should be clear, at this point in this chapter, what the mind-set of the author is and, perhaps, to what conclusion it may lead. The consensually accepted means of discussion and possible proof being used here in the author-reader dialogue is logical thought, reasonable discourse carried on through the medium of printed symbols. The implicit assumption on the part of the participants is that the dialectical use of reason and logic is a valid means of demonstrating proof. One should be aware at least that what we take as the normal mode of reasoning has been influenced, even altered, by historical events that are the direct result of the application of theological criteria. As De Bono has pointed out,

(the dialectical mode of thought is) the Greek idiom redesigned by the

(the dialectical mode of thought is) the Greek idiom redesigned by the Church in the Middle Ages . . . an extremely inefficient mode for change because its original purpose was to repress change.

Church in the Middle Ages. The dialectic, adversarial system is an extremely inefficient mode for change because its original purpose was to repress change. It was designed by medieval scholastic philosophers to destroy heretics. . . . In the Church view, it was a perfectly correct idiom because if you accepted the same basic premises, then the dialectic wordplay could "prove" something wrong or right, inconsistent or consistent. For that purpose it was perfectly valid, but in many other areas, where perceptions differ and people change it is very detrimental.[22]

Even if we agree that it will be the individual reader's subjective judgement, certainly, that is exercised in evaluating the information presented here, one can easily perceive how riddled with assumptions and subjective criteria even that statement is! The epistemic barrier is itself at least partially a product of our cultural evolution. But my purpose here is to point out the relativities of Western thinking rather than enter into a discourse on the subtleties of philosophy. It will be sufficient if I have made it clear that the foundation of the theological criterion is itself brought into question here, the philosophical criterion has at least been molded by the influence of the theological criterion and the scientific criterion, also having developed at least partially as a reaction to both the theological and the philosophical approach, is too limited. We must determine by what criteria we will judge while, at the same time, reevaluating the criteria that we use as a possible product of a cultural heritage which is now being questioned as to its accuracy!

Our metaphoric progress that has seen us discover more and more minutely how we function and what precisely we are is, in a much broader sense, another form of the pervasive feedback loops in which we are involved. The process of self-discovery has given rise, over the span of our history, to temporarily adequate explanations of what we are and what our situation is all about. We call this our philosophy and the criteria we have adopted for the accuracy and veracity of those explanations has always been the language developed as an expression of the type of awareness which we were or are investigating most intensely at any given time; we use, as our criteria, the highest function of our consciousness that we can reflexively consensually identify. A salient feature of our metamorphosis is that our criteria are evolving as we are; we will develop better criteria to the degree

The demand here is not just for reevaluating the entirety of our past and present cultural history but for no less than creating a new philosophical and social global order.

that we are conscious of that process.

But we will inevitably turn, as philotropic humans at this stage of our metamorphosis, to the most fundamental, generic, common basis for human agreement and consensus, the subjective cogency of the evidence—repeat, at this stage of our evolution/metamorphosis.

Because the pattern of evidence from archaeology has become so strong, so clear, so obvious.

Because disconnected enigmas, puzzles, loose ends and contradictions in so many areas dovetail together and are subsumed by the archaeological evidence so fully in such an elegantly meaningful and logical way that the cogent overview totally overshadows any other explanation.

Because, when we ask the ultimate existential question Why has it been this way and not one of some innumerable other ways . . .

One need only open one's mind to the undeniable existence of the ancient cities, the volumes of records of the discoveries of ooparts, the items of advanced technology seemingly out of place in history, to become at least curious. But only when one gives fair hearing to the translations and ultimately to the fact that only in the context delineated by Sitchin does the entirety of our beginnings, our creation, our mysteriously sophisticated, precocious ancient past, our amazingly uniform global "legends," our relatively meteoric metamorphic progress, our obsessive drive for self-comprehension and transcendence, the off-planet home-seeking thrust of our future orientation, become coherently and imminently intelligible. I ask only that the reader maintain a level of awareness that allows one to be constantly aware of the influence of criteria which are themselves brought into question by the very information under discussion and to question their silent authority. The subtle fear experienced when considering the ramifications of this new view will be a constant obstacle until we see clearly that the cultural, religious, and scientific biases we have are a function of or a reaction to the self-perpetuating dogmas that claim it is an offense to question them.

We all recognize that, collectively, we are moving toward a more and more relativistic mode of thought. We recognize with less clarity that epistemology is a function of the type or mode of awareness, consciousness,

But we leave a mode when its language and its explanations are no longer adequate, when its limits are reached, when we can imagine, glimpse, grasp, experience what is beyond.

---

in which one happens to be operating. One tends to become insecure when the hooks into the consensual or private reality one has been accustomed to become loosened enough to threaten the validity of that very reality—and the demand here is not only for reevaluating the entirety of our past and present cultural history but for no less than creating a new philosophical and social global order. I am well aware that is like asking the bees to radically rethink their hive. The process can be quite unsettling or it can be a tremendous source of challenge and opportunity for personal expansion. But we leave a mode when its language and its explanations are no longer adequate, when its limits are reached, when we can imagine, glimpse, grasp, experience what is beyond that mode and its inaccuracies and its mind-set. We create context by dealing with problems of thought, build context in the effort to surmount obstacles and it is the nature of the context itself which furnishes the clues as to how to transcend it.

I will have succeeded if I will have opened up the vision of what it will be like to know our real beginnings and become no longer robot slaves to a primitive world view but our own intelligent masters, the selectors of our own criteria, the creators of our own reality.

In descending order of importance, listed below are three major items which demand verification and/or further exploration.

The location of the planet Nibiru, the home planet of the Nefilim and the last one to be discovered in our solar system, being sought by Charles Kowal of Palomar Observatory, the Naval Observatory and for which the Voyager space craft have been used to triangulate.

Verification of the history of the solar system's formation and the subsequent collisional events detailed in the ancient documents. This could best be accomplished by extending the system of microcomputers, each dedicated to simulating the motion and characteristics of a single planet, run in parallel (a digital orrery) in order to project the solar system's history backward and forward as developed by Gerald Sussman of MIT or the use of a powerful mainframe computer with sufficient speed. The work of Napier and Clube of the Royal Observatory in Scotland and Ovenden of Canada may also contribute significantly in this area. Serious observation in visual telescope work has already been done by Kowal, the Naval Observatory and others.

Vast amount of research is demanded by or will be stimulated by the new view of human nature. We need to get on with the process.

Genetic clues that would indicate genetic engineering between Homo Erectus and Nefilim. These might be found in the area of or give clues to the reason for the unique cleft in our upper lip, our hairless, rich-in-sweat-glands type of skin, our turned down nose, etc. The most recent scientific information we have obtained from the work especially in DNA "fingerprinting," the application of restrictive enzymes to DNA to pinpoint mutations, and the work being done in the area of both nuclear and mitochondrial DNA comparison show several preliminary findings of direct interest: there is strong indication that Cro-Magnon man did not evolve from Neanderthal; in addition to a migration of Homo-Erectus out of Africa into Europe and most of Asia, there is evidence of a major migration of our species on the order of 50,000 to 30,000 years ago; the combined findings of the most advanced techniques and the fossil evidence would point to a single source for humans as we know ourselves somewhere around 200,000 years ago. Sitchin's analysis would point to 300,000 years ago and it remains to be seen how accurate either estimate will prove to be.

A vast amount of research is demanded by or will be stimulated by the new view of human nature. We need to get on with the process.

CHAPTER 7
SENSE AND SUBLIMATION

"The Lutheran church has always been based on the Bible," explains Phil Beck, Production Manager of a local paint company and the superintendent of the Church's Sunday School. "If you start questioning it, where do you stop? If I have to have that much education to sit down and understand *Genesis*, then why did God let Luther put it in the people's language? At what point do I throw the whole mad mess out the door?"

Time Magazine

Following the wrong god home, we have seen all of those we did not understand as alien, the enemy. Failing to comprehend each other's politics, cultures, and subcultures, which often are based on a different worldview, we questioned each other's motives . . . denied each other's humanity.[23]

Marilyn Ferguson

You've got to pick up every stitch . . .

Supersession

In the last fifteen years we have learned more about the formation of the cosmos, the galaxies, the solar system than in the entire time we have been even aware of those subjects. We have traced the origins of the universe all the way back to the first few milliseconds after the so-called Big Bang. As a result we have gradually and rather dispassionately divested ourselves of the true myths, the naive, picturesque explanations of the formation of the cosmos, the solar system, the earth. But how long have we listened to the stories of how "God created" mankind without understanding what that really means? The choices regarding the interpretation of that statement no longer are limited to an acceptance, on blind faith, of a hands-on concocting of a human being out of mud or a torturous and embarrassed academic explanation of Genesis as literary and poetic metaphors created by simple minds or an outright rejection on the basis of a perplexity that impatiently throws out the Old Testament whole. Although the archaeological evidence and the body of what history has been preserved from the ancient times, viewed in the perspective afforded by the level of technological knowledge we have now attained, show clearly that the religions and philosophies based on a misinterpretation and/or sublimation of that

101

Although transmuting the massive structure of religions, would appear, at first, as an impossible and even preposterous task, there is a way that it may be accomplished.

information are obsolete, a monumental problem lies in making the transition that will phase them out. It is greater than phasing out the flat-earth or geo-centric theories, greater than any planetary paradigm shift that we have known in our history. It is one thing to lose face by having to accept a heliocentric explanation of the solar system as the Christian church has had to do over time or to have to publicly "apologize" to Galileo after all this time. It is another matter entirely to have to face the prospect of literally "going out of business" as an institutionalized religion. The depth of the historical roots, the investment in influence and power, political clout, the claim to divine authorization, the ability to intimidate and repress members, the staggering size of the organizational structure, the problem of who would take the initiative, the potential psychological trauma suffered by those who can not or will not understand, the lack of perspective as to how to gracefully rise to a new level of humanity, are all obstacles. **But the change is even more inevitable than it is, apparently, tremendously difficult.**

Although transmuting the massive structure of religions, taken as a collective whole on the planet, into a positive force for the achievement of the next plateau of our metamorphosis would appear, at first, as an impossible and even preposterous task, there is a way that it may be accomplished. We must first recognize that the perceptions of the three broad classifications of the parts of the phenomenon called religion have already begun to change subtly in the common consciousness.

The following discussion constitutes an outline, a primer of transmutation, of transition.

We identify three main phases of the phenomenon called religion on this planet.

1. **institutional religion**: formal organizations with leaders and members, rules of membership, organization, approved doctrine, moral codes, rituals of worship, historical tradition.

2. **transcendent experience**: personal subjective experience of a type of consciousness, a mode of awareness of, and/or a physical and/or mental contact with a personal or impersonal power beyond what one understands oneself to be, within or without an institutional context.

The purpose here is to sort out the various parts of the entire phenomenon known as religion so that each may be seen for what it really is and dealt with separately.

---

3. **the occult:** that nebulous body of puzzling, often secret, doctrines concerning esoteric knowledge, professing to hold keys to transcendent levels of mind, experience and being through learning, rituals, magic.

To anticipate questions and/or objections on the part of the reader:

a. yoga as a systematic technique to gain control over autonomic bodily functions, mental discipline, self-control I classify precisely and only as such; yoga techniques that are specifically designed to produce mind-altering, mind-expanding or transcendent experience I include under the second category above, transcendent experience.

b. The occult is included under the general heading of religion on the basis that some occult tradition at least is within the specific context of a religion as, for example, the Kabbala (Cabala, Quabbala) is within the Hebrew tradition.

c. all classification here is fully recognized as the subjective judgement of the author just as the author fully recognizes the subjective judgement of the reader whose typical question may be How can you say transcendent experience is open to anyone when only persons in good standing in my religion can have direct experience of God? The difficulty here is also typical: the reader raising this type of objection usually is reluctant to admit that her or his judgement is subjective, citing divine authority of some sort. One may ask by what criterion that person judges that the divine authority is infallible or at least that the human transmitter from whom he or she has received the information that the divine source is indeed divine and/or infallible is to be believed. As we have seen, in the previous chapter, the Achilles' heel of all argument based on reason is that one may continue to ask the same question as to what criterion of truth has been used to judge the veracity of whatever criterion is advanced. Most discussions of this nature lead nowhere; the best one can ask for, as a rule, is an agreement to disagree in a friendly fashion.

d. an objection that organized religions should not be included since they are only organizations and true religion is essentially personal experience can only be answered the same way as the previous objection.

The purpose here is to sort out the various parts of the entire phenomenon known as religion so that each may be seen for what it really is

The most fundamental significance of the consciousness revolution of the 1960's was that it was established beyond doubt that anyone who wished could explore the highest "religious" and "mystical" experience at will.

and dealt with separately, for each area is changing and must change in its own unique way.

Transcendent experience and the occult are already being transmuted by the processes of gradual reinterpretation and redefinition.

One of the most important products of our search for self-understanding is the reflexive analysis of transcendent experience, the generic manifestation of the leading edge of our metamorphic progress. Although the common consciousness is only gradually coming to assimilate it, the area of mysticism and transcendent experience has been definitively redefined as neuro-psychological, in terms of expanded consciousness and probing of new dimensions of energy frequencies. It has been shown to be a general area of activity of the human brain/neurological system having well defined levels. As discussed in the previous chapter, throughout our history we have record of the gradual development of techniques, systems of training and psychoactive drugs that can be used to expand consciousness and intelligence. Against the background of the accumulated neurological findings, the psychedelic chemicals originally attracted the interest of the pioneer researchers as psychologists in the 1960s because of their potential for behavior change under the control of the subject rather than by the externally applied conditioning methods used by Skinner and others. The broader outcome was that it soon became very clear that an individual could create any reality-tunnel that she or he wished and could alter and improve her or his own behavior even to the extent of re-imprinting. The most fundamental significance of the consciousness revolution of the 1960s was that it was established beyond doubt that anyone could explore any area of human consciousness at will (including the highest "religious" and "mystical" experiences), by using certain psychedelic drugs. Consciousness was conclusively demonstrated to be neurological. Several vectors of thought came together at that point. The philosophical principles that had found expression in Berkeley's subjectivism came to full realization. The adoption of the vocabulary of physics by psychedelic researchers to express the spectrum of human awareness, particularly that of the transcendental, integrated the disciplines of Psychology and Physics. The epistemological debates concerning the nature of reality and truth were recast into an even more complicated dimension since the

Transcendent experience is clearly the most profound, essential, intelligent and advanced human activity: the leading edge of the metamorphic process.

philosophical statements **about** objectivity and subjectivity were now put under the microscope of the direct neurological experience of the processes of perception, processing and judging. The relativistic concepts of Einsteinian physics were seen to express the subjective nature of our perception of "objective" truth and reality.

The result of this redefinition is twofold: it separates organized religion and transcendent experience and the occult and yet, although at first it seems to eliminate the concept of the "religious experience," it clarifies just what the objective of our metamorphic process is all about. The process of intelligence increase takes us unerringly into a deeper and deeper understanding of the totality of reality, the universe, unified field theories, the ultimate causes of even the universe or an infinite number of universes. This searching impels us to seek not only information **about** ultimate answers but **direct experience** of the most profound and fundamental levels of which we are capable and unity, fusion with other intelligences which we can recognize. This is not a reductionistic process; the redefinition actually expands the generic concept of "religious"—in the sense of seeking the knowledge and experience of ultimate reality and the cause of it—and removes it from the cramping narrowness and limitations of divisive doctrinal proprietariness. Transcendent experience is clearly the most profound, essential, intelligent and advanced human activity: the leading edge of the metamorphic process. Although we tend to use traditional terminology, "experience" in this case must be expanded to include both knowledge and the direct neurological processes. One cannot seek what one does not have a clue about and one cannot communicate and understand what one has experienced unless there is a data-base used as a reference and/or which can furnish at least the fundamental elements for an adequate language to express it. The decade of the 60's furnishes a classic example. The sudden strong interest in the ancient teachings of the East is easily understood in this context since the "spiritual" disciplines of the East are primarily neuro-psychological and are designed to move the consciousness of the practitioner through specific phases of neuro-genetic metamorphosis. In that revolutionary period the West rediscovered three great texts of the East: the *I Ching*, the *Tibetan Book of the Dead*, and the *Book of the Tao*. The *I Ching* teaches one how to tread the variables, to be in harmony with constant change and live gracefully high at the level of opposites. The *Book of the Dead* is

Within and without the religions of the world there has always been, over the centuries, an "underground"; it is called the occult tradition. It is in a state of total shambles.

a psychological "Baedeker," a guide book of transition through the Hessian tourist traps as one moves from the level of opposites through the transitional detachments to the levels of highest energies; its proper language is that of relativistic physics. The *Book of the Tao* teaches one how to operate from the cosmic, creatorial perspective, beyond opposites; its proper language is that of quantum physics. Those who instinctively recognized the relevance of those texts but who were not able to make or refused to recognize the connection to the more adequate advanced languages of modern physics tend to recycle within the framework of outmoded models. The metamorphic momentum is impeded by loss of orientation to the stimulus of future possibles. That which we transcend are the limitations of consensual "reality," our personal and collective games, the parameters of our current vision and experience. The only activity that we can pursue without satiation, boredom or being confronted with limits is intelligence increase which is best implemented through the conscious pursuit of transcendent experience.

Within and without the religions of the world there has always been, over the centuries, an "underground": it is called the occult tradition. It is in a state of total shambles. The occult, considered abstractly, is a puzzling phenomenon encompassing a number of subjects but having, as its common thread, roots in the ancient past and an esoteric, enigmatic character. Within the span of the sense of the dictionary definition as "matters regarded as involving the action or influence of supernatural or supernormal powers or some secret knowledge of them" (Webster) have been included everything in the spectrum between evil and the divine. History shows that the occult has been dabbled in or seriously practiced by everyone from laymen to scientists, philosophers, and even at least one Pope. The tangled history of the occult also includes witches, magicians, alchemists, sorcerers, astrologers, diviners, practitioners of the I Ching, the Tarot, the Kabbala, as well as seers and those with extrasensory tendencies, depending on the mood, prejudices, and orientation of the times in which they lived. The domain of the occult is difficult to define in so far as one person's unquestioned religious belief may be another person's philosophical postulate or another person's occult practice; what is cosmic principle to one may be a charlatan's conceit to another.

We may ask the question Why has the phenomenon of the occult

The area of the occult will be redefined as the preserved content of advanced technological, scientific and psychological information given to us by Nefilim.

tradition been with us so tenaciously for so long and survived in spite of the criticism of the scientist and the theologian. The pat answer is that humans need that element of the mysterious in their psychology and often accept it irrationally. But, as we have already seen with regard to the persistence of what were pronounced myth and legend concerning the existence of ancient cities, kings and civilizations until audacious explorers actually dug them up, a tradition that survives through the ages often has a core element that sustains it. One might almost draw a rule of thumb from the manner in which that occurrence typically has repeated itself over the centuries. The most general and spectacular case is obviously exemplified in the way the "legends" and "myths" concerning our beginnings persisted until the accumulated archaeological evidence was finally illuminated by the discoveries (genetic engineering, electronics, lasers, space flight) of our latest level of technology.

Even taking into account the attractiveness of the mysterious in times of heavy rational orientation and the seductiveness of secret power, there is a core content in the perennial tradition that exhibits a magnetism for those predisposed to seek expansion of awareness and understanding. It is at that point that formal religion, mysticism, defined as a seeking of transcendent experience of dimensions beyond the normal, and the occult overlap. And it is at that point that the processes of reinterpretation and redefinition have begun to operate due to our having attained a level of psychological, technological and scientific expertise that allows us to explain phenomena as well as recognize an historical base for them.

The area of the genuine occult will be redefined as the preserved content of advanced technological, scientific and psychological information given to us by the Nefilim with the injunction, at least in some cases, to preserve it until we reached a level of expertise that would enable us to decode and understand it. It has been surrounded with ritual and ceremony, just as organized religion surrounds doctrine with liturgy, to enhance its importance and to preserve its integrity. An intense re-examination of the field, spurred by the recognition of the real nature of the occult, will gradually identify that core content and sort it out from the subsequent accretions of lesser material added over time. I can only outline the vast area and suggest possible approaches; it will take the work of many experts in individual areas to accomplish the task. The redefinition is based on the

The new archaeological perspective provides us finally with a possible plausible base for the existence and enigmatic nature of the occult.

confluence of the new archaeological perspective with technological discoveries in very recent times. The archaeological evidence allows us to understand how humans received high technological information and training in times when we had formerly assumed we were primitive: the Nefilim gave us information and training, at least to certain selected groups. This is the root source of ooparts, the out-of-place-in-time artifacts that have been a source of mystery for so long. It also establishes a plausible base for the traditions of the occult although the mysterious character of the information handed down by that tradition seems to stem from the fact that the information entrusted was not always understood by its human recipients and was intended by the Nefilim to be preserved until we could decode it: timed-release capsules of technological information.

We can now discern some possible interpretations of specific occult practices. Within this context of reinterpretation there are five general bases for types of the occult. The principles, practices and rituals

1. were based on **copying** what was originally understood when it was transmitted to us but the understanding of which has been lost over time.

2. were simply a **mimicking** of technology or customs which were witnessed long ago, recognized as powerful or important but never understood and perhaps were never intended for us or even prohibited to us.

3. were **entrusted to us for decoding in the future** but never understood for what they were but have been simply handed down in a carefully preserved form because we were ordered under pain of severe penalty for failure to do so.

4. were actually **invented by humans** some time after contact with the Nefilim had begun to fade and based on human experience with experimentation.

5. were some **combination** of the above.

Against that background, I submit some tentative evaluations of the various forms of the occult without apology. These remarks are only intended to stimulate discussion and investigation. Vast amounts of accumulated dross must be stripped away. The general character of the potential information already emerging comes from the level of physical

The inference can easily be drawn that the occult Cabala tradition is a clear case of advanced knowledge being given as a package for full decipherment in the future.

reality that is a type which will explicate the next developments in the areas which now constitute the leading edge of our science. This is simply the converse of the fact that our science has only now allowed us to understand the nature of the potential information in the first place. There may be information that is still too advanced for our current conceptual framework.

The new paradigm will open up scientific possibilities in four general areas of science. (Noorbergen's work on ooparts becomes an encyclopedia of possible leads in the new perspective.)

In the area of physics, a single representative example: the tachyon field energy (Tesla, Moray, Feinberg, Nieper, Brown, Seike, et.al.) just now entering our field of comprehension, seems to have been understood and used by the Nefilim. Evidence comes from such disparate areas as Australia where the aborigines use the *turingas*, lines of force which they claim were reshaped by "the creative gods" in the "dream time"; the Chinese have used the *lung-mei*, the "dragon currents"; the modern Druids claim their forefathers knew enough about them to use them to levitate great weight and even for flight, etc. These lines are marked over the entire globe by stone markers from England to the Sahara to Australia apparently planted in a single coordinated survey.

In mathematics/"natural" languages: An example is the recent discovery, by Stan Tenen (Meru Foundation, San Anselmo, CA),[24] that the character set of the Hebrew alphabet can be generated on a flat surface by using a shadow box technique, shining a light on a unique three dimensional asymmetrical ribbon form as it is rotated through a specific sequence. The ribbon form represents one and three-quarter turns around the 2-torus generated by rotating a tetrahedron. This demonstrates that someone, far back in history, had knowledge of the basic geometry of three dimensional space in the same terms put forth by the visionary Buckminster Fuller and which is still being developed by mathematicians today. It demonstrates a deliberate structuring of a "natural" language based on fundamental physical principles facilitating communication and self-correction through common universal elements. Since it is clear, in the new view, that the Hebrew tradition traces its source directly to the Nefilim, the inference can easily be drawn that the occult Cabala tradition is a case of advanced knowledge being given as a package for full decipherment in the future. This does not rule out the possibility that there were humans that

The research now being carried out on longevity and immortality should be able to benefit from the information contained in the ancient records.

understood it fully at one time in the past but the keys to it have apparently been lost over time. The Hebrew alphabet characters have always been attributed multi-level special meaning in the Cabalistic teachings. Further computer work on the subject may provide keys to fundamental information that will dovetail with and implement a wide range of investigations in mathematics and physics and also have application in the field of computer languages.

The roots of what has come down to us as the Free Mason geometric tradition possibly springs from an application, well exemplified in the Nefilim constructed original pyramids, related to this fundamental "natural" language of mathematical/physical principles.

The area of biology/genetics: the research now being carried out on longevity and immortality should be able to benefit from the information contained in the ancient records concerning the nature of the plant products that the Nefilim seem to have used for their own purposes in that area. Longevity was definitely associated with a plant growing in the sea in shallow enough water for a human to dive for it without special gear. Other references may yield themselves to careful analysis by biologists and archaeologists and linguists working together.

The area of astronomy: the detailed account of the formation of the solar system contained in the documents already translated (see Sitchin's interpretation and analysis in *The Twelfth Planet*, chap. 7) should furnish detailed information to the solar system astronomer. Diligent study may also yield the key to the as yet indecipherable formulae for calculating distances between stars and other items found in the ancient astronomical texts.

The *I Ching*, the revered book of oracles coming out of a six thousand year old Chinese tradition, has a source shrouded in the mists of the valleys of the Yellow River's ancient past. The theme of ancestor worship and the references to the gods it contains and which is so much a part of the Chinese tradition takes on a new meaning if we see the Nefilim "gods" as the original "ancestors." The traditions surrounding it speak of an ancient personage, Fu Hsi, as the inventor of the linear signs. A fundamental concept at root of its system is that there is no steady state, the only permanent thing is change. The deliberately adopted basis of the system of hexagrams that mirror the constantly changing patterns of human psychology is **chance** which, it is

The mechanisms contained in the Book of Changes will fall within the realm of the new conceptualization of "chance" which shows that there is order found in chaos and geometric form in randomness

claimed, maximizes communication/contact with suprahuman intelligence. The subtlety and depth of knowledge of human psychology contained in the book has not been surpassed until the present. It is difficult to conceive of such concepts coming from any other source than some individuals who had access to an advanced knowledge base as the legends claim. When translated into modern mathematical and physics terms, as has been partially done by the McKenna[25] brothers who traced the various cycles contained therein by computer analysis, it seems most likely that the mechanisms contained in the Book of Changes will fall within the realm of the new conceptualization of "chance" developed by Prigogine, and the work being done by Abraham, Shaw, Cruthfield, Farmer, Packard and others which shows that there is order found in chaos and there is an underlying geometric form in randomness. These statements concerning the I Ching are speculative on my part although I see sufficient indicators, as yet without rigorous verification, to convince me of at least the urgency for those with specialization in the field to undertake an in-depth investigation. Although the I Ching is outmoded for the areas of highest consciousness (just as in Physics, other "laws" dominate at the relativistic and quantum levels) of which we already have considerable direct experience, fundamental patterns of human psychology up to the level of the socio-sexual imprint are dealt with in the I Ching in subtle detail. The variables within sixty-four gestalt-like hexagrams are defined and, if one or more change within a given configuration, the resultant configuration is predictable. This does not negate freedom of choice, ingenuity or the ability to transcend those four circuits; it actually should encourage individuals to do so.

A curious bit of this has possibly been done incidentally by Robert Prechter "the hottest forecaster (stock market) in the Free World" who has won the United States Trading Championship four years running and commands premium money for his consultations by using a computerized form of prediction based on Elliott wave theory. Prechter and Elliott wave theory say that predictable waves, rhythms of investor **psychology**, not interest rates, earnings or prices, is the prime moving force behind stock-market cycles, that those patterns repeat themselves following the well-known Fibonacci series; humans do not act randomly. Six thousand or more years ago the I Ching was saying the same thing.

The fragmented tradition of healing with the use of crystals, gem stones, light may have its origins in a mimicking or copying of Nefilim practices that apparently were a form of medical technology.

Alchemy, in the way it is popularly understood, seems a pseudo-science practiced by early experimenters without sufficient information and with grandiose intent to transmute base metals into gold. The initiated often claim subtler levels that are psychological rather than physical. Mercury is mentioned in the ancient texts, both Western and Eastern, related to power sources for flight. The alloys and metals mentioned in the Tibetan manuscripts that are still unknown to us may have been made by the Nefilim in the vacuum of space just as we are experimenting to achieve now. The Nefilim had reached a state of technology that included some sort of atomic power according to the accounts of their wars and therefore knew of transmutation of elements. If there is a solid core to alchemy (its "beginnings" in 410 A.D. more a surfacing) it might lie, not in the spells and incantations associated with it, but in a copying or simple mimicking of misunderstood chemical technology or smelting and refining techniques that the Nefilim used to process the large quantities of gold they mined.

The fragmented tradition of healing with the use of crystals, gem stones, light, and the ancient customs of wearing certain amulets etc. may have its origins in a mimicking or copying of Nefilim practices described in the ancient records that apparently were a form of medical technology possibly similar to the latest use of light, lasars, special wavelengths of light and other frequencies of radiation for curative purposes and the use of crystals as is being investigated by Voegel. If it is proven that there is substance in this view then the possibility of accelerating our knowledge rapidly in these areas is opened up.

The Nefilim engaged in extensive space flight and there is a tendency for those coming in contact with this subject matter to make an immediate connection between them and the UFO phenomenon. Although it is true that the stories related in the Old Testament concerning the rides into space given to certain humans were probably in rocket-technology vehicles, there is no obvious explicit link to the advanced craft that are usually reported as UFOs. Regardless whether one assigns the phenomenon of UFOs to the classification of the occult, the scientific or the supranormal, in view of the evidence that the Nefilim were already capable of space travel 450,000 years ago and at least 300,000 years technologically in advance of us, we should at least allow the possibility that what we are witnessing is simply the periodic direct or robot monitoring of this planet. We never were considered more than

Immortality was a relative physical immortality for the Nefilim and, over time, there was a sublimation of that concept into the life-after-death human traditions and rituals.

high-level "lab animals" by the Nefilim; we may still be considered an on-going experiment. Dealing with that situation may be a matter of very serious concern to us as a race sooner than we might anticipate. This would be, perhaps, the simplest explanation of the phenomenon if it is real. Visitation from other places and races is not ruled out but is outside of the subject of this book.

The Hermetic tradition is based on Gnostic writings and teachings appearing in the first three centuries A.D. and which that tradition attributes to Hermes Trimegistus. The Gnostics taught that matter is evil and salvation could only come through a knowledge of esoteric spiritual truths. Hermes Trismegistus (the thrice greatest) was the Greek title for the god Thoth whom they identified as the god Hermes. Hermes Trismegistus is held to be a "legendary" figure in the usual academic framework but Origen, Clement, and Augustine looked to him as a valid basis for their *apologies* (apologia: a defense of one's opinion, actions, position). When one reads the translations of the writings attributed to Hermes Trismegistus, particularly the instructions to his son concerning humans, one is at first struck by the peculiar sense of separation, the almost alien point of view that comes through so strongly in Hermes' attitude toward humans which he is obviously attempting to inculcate in his son. It is at least like a disdainful monarch speaking about subjects whom he considers to be very inferior indeed. When one re-reads those words in the new perspective in which the Nefilim gods are recognized as humanoid and real, however, it seems quite clear that we have in hand the actual words of a Nefilim god instructing his young son as to how to relate to and deal with their human slaves. Although he emphasizes the fact that humans are very limited and sometimes border on depravity it is clear that he and his son are entirely different and not even subject to the laws that govern humans. In the new view the hermetic tradition would be a private educational data-bank and it is perhaps the most clear-cut and recent document directly from a Nefilim source that we possess. The elements of the magical, the alchemical and the astrological contained in that body of information may eventually be seen to be otherwise in a way similar to that in which the Cabalistic treatment of the Hebrew alphabet has begun to change.

Immortality is a dominant theme woven through the subject of religion, philosophy and the entire subject of the occult in its many varied forms. It

Over and above physical immortality, which appears already as potentially genetically achievable by our science, did the Nefilim themselves have a philosophy of mind, a "religious" orientation?

takes on both the form of a belief in the indefinite continuation of a spirit/soul after death as well as in a dimension in which consciousness forms exist on a non-material level.

Immortality is defined differently within different theological, philosophical and occult contexts. Doctrines such as the Hindu and the Christian teach that immortality cannot be avoided and comes after the death of the body but the Hindu teaches that the soul, the spiritual part, recycles through karmically determined states while the Christian teaches that the body will be reunited with the soul at a certain point and that there is no recycling. To be precise, many of the early thinkers of the Christian religion, even those respected as Fathers of the Church, have taught a variety of approaches to the subject and there have been variations of the doctrine within Christianity which have been officially "eliminated" over time. But the occult traditions also contain well-defined and developed teachings concerning the nature of immortality even to the extent of purporting to communicate with or "channelling" those entities, both human souls and non-human spirits, who, it is claimed, exist in the non-material realm.

If one asks the question Why is there such a strong focus on immortality in the religious and occult traditions of the world, the answer, in the new archaeological perspective, is quite clear: immortality was a relative physical immortality for the Nefilim and, over time, there was a sublimation of that concept into the life-after-death human traditions and rituals found within both organized religion and the occult traditions. The desire to achieve that same immortality has haunted humans from our beginning; a handful, by the records, have actually been granted it.

But there is another dimension to the subject that is the most intriguing and tantalizing part of the entire subject of our beginnings, our "training," our metamorphosis and our future direction: over and above physical immortality, which appears already as potentially genetically achievable by our science, did the Nefilim themselves have a philosophy of mind, a "religious" orientation, use techniques to expand their consciousness, seek a transcendent reality, have proof, perhaps hard empirical data, of existence of consciousness on a level beyond the material? If so did they teach that information to us as part of the "crash-course" in civilization they gave us? There are a number of threads that must be untangled before we can see clearly what the answer to that question might be.

Their physical immortality is consistently and explicitly related to an ingested substance.

Their orientation does not seem to fit either of the current religious or occult mind-sets as generally extant. It does appear that the Nefilim were at a level of sophistication philosophically at which we find ourselves today at least in certain elements of our population. It also seems quite clear that their concepts of the transcendent were linked to their scientific knowledge as ours is increasingly becoming and I find no evidence for a tradition of the occult, in the fundamental sense of a hidden teaching, as such among the Nefilim. (One of the reasons we have an occult tradition, over and above the fact that some of the information was perhaps originally beyond our comprehension in the first place, is the practical issue of the survival of those who were attempting to preserve those teachings in the face of competition from Catholic Christianity. The bitter combat in the first centuries A.D. was not only intellectual. The death penalty was in force at various times for adherence to Gnostic doctrines which were within the Church itself as well as outside of it. That Gnosticism went underground to be hidden is quite understandable.) The evidence which is available clearly depicts them as technologically and scientifically oriented; they were here for the purpose of mining, played very heavy political games among themselves and seemed to "worship" nothing above them. Making allowances for the fact that their most advanced thinking may not have been available to humans for a number of reasons, there is the possibility that they had a developed philosophy or psychology of which we are not aware; they may even have established contact with extraterrestrial civilizations whom they revered as far more advanced on a scientific basis as we are seeking to do now for all we know. If there was a contact between the Nefilim and another civilization the knowledge humans acquired of it may be showing up in the doggedly Sirius pursuit of certain fragments of the "occult" traditions. And all we may deduce about that part of their thinking may be (*maybe*) what the most knowledgeable among us concerning the "occult" traditions can tell us of the sources they can trace of the most powerful of the practices. It is well to keep in mind that, from one perspective, a great deal of human knowledge about the Nefilim is akin to the backstairs gossip of servants—which we were. I suggest that we will find, eventually, that all of the extraordinary, synchronistic, meta-scientific phenomena that constitute the most potent of the traditions we know will be found to be advanced science.

It should become increasingly clear that their relative physical immortality,

The doctrine of metempsychosis, the cyclical reincarnation of the individual soul, does appear woven through the most ancient traditions we know from all parts of the world.

coupled with the ability to completely repair damage and/or to restore life after accidental—or deliberate—injury or death could put immortality after death in a somewhat less essential or urgent perspective. Their physical immortality is consistently and explicitly related to an ingested substance. There is record of pressure to conform being put on a member of their high council by threat of withholding that substance. Their collective orientation, therefore, seems quite clearly to have been an integrated, scientifically orientated view of the universe that did not divide reality into natural and supernatural as our traditions have. The teachings, admonitions and codes of social ethics as well as the highly detailed training instructions on how to serve their masters written down in the ancient records—right down to the fine detail of a recipe for chicken cooked in wine—and in the Old Testament do not give indication of a Nefilim religion. They are exclusively concerned with the proper conduct of humans as little more than slaves. What has been interpreted as high religious doctrine in human interpretation is really a celebration or praising of the characteristics and deeds of the Nefilim masters as humas have praised their rulers—willingly or unwillingly.

But, having said all that, the doctrine of immortality or more specifically that of metempsychosis, the cyclical reincarnation of the individual soul, does appear woven through the most ancient traditions we know from all parts of the world. There is a doctrine of metempsychosis in the writings of Thoth-Hermes. If Thoth-Hermes (Egyptian center) was Nefilm as the evidence indicates then there is ground for identifying such doctrine as held by and coming directly from the Nefilim. If it were a prevalent doctrine among the Nefilim then its existence in the Indian center where Ishtar ruled is logical. The Cabala teachings coming, it is believed, from the earliest Mesopotamian Nefilim center and transmitted through the Hebrew tribe contain the doctrine. Although it might be concluded, in view of the possible Nefilim source of such a doctrine, that therefore it is a very advanced and significant one to which we should give credence, I do not agree. I submit that we should evaluate that doctrine in the light of the Nefilim's stage of intellectual development many thousand of years ago as accurately as we can ascertain from the evidence and also take into consideration the unique personal characteristics of the Nefilim individuals who may have transmitted it to us. At this point I see the following possibilities with regard to the concept of metempsychosis:

The personal proclivities of the individual Nefilim personalities colored and formed the traditions of the humans who were under their control in specific areas of the world over which they had dominion.

1. It was and is a misinterpretation and sublimation of advanced practices of cloning techniques, techniques of life extension or the actual relative immortality of the Nefilim themselves on the part of humans.

2. It was a popular doctrine held philosophically by the Nefilim who were at a stage of development approximately equivalent to ours today and which they were not able, at that stage, to either prove or disprove conclusively. Humans may have casually acquired it or been taught it by the Nefilim in this form.

3. Reincarnation may be a fact. If so it is amenable to eventual scientific verification and probably control. The Nefilim may have reached a point at which it was an established scientific phenomenon which they took for granted. Humans may have casually acquired knowledge of it or been taught it by the Nefilim in this form. There appears to be a clear source in the Nefilim doctrines for metempsychosis: the words of Hermes Trismegistus are a good example. But that does not make it, *ipso facto*, scientific law.

The Nefilim mentality in those times quite clearly approximates to the well-educated mentality of today; that is the reason why we can finally understand them and the technology they possessed. But just as that technology seems so comfortable and familiar to us today so does their philosophy seem no more advanced than ours is currently. In view of that similarity I strongly urge that we view their thinking in the context of their evolutionary development and recognize that they may have had no more or less a criteria base and verification for such doctrines than we. I would be very curious as to where their thinking has taken them at this point rather than identify them with the thinking we may have record of thousands of years ago. And that thinking seems to vary from one Nefilim personality to another just as ours does.

A key to understanding the varieties of human traditions is found in the psychology of the individual Nefilim. The picture that emerges from the ancient history is one in which the personal proclivities of the individual Nefilim personalities colored and formed the traditions of the humans who were under their control in specific areas of the world over which they had dominion. As pointed out earlier, our Western culture has been predominantly formed on the basis of the tradition of one tribe, in one location, under one

We can already see the root source of the gradually ritualized elements of Tantra, the sexual yoga, in the influence and practices of Ishtar.

Nefilim personality, ultimately a very narrow set of parameters. Contrast the remote, peevish, exacting and quite ruthless Yahweh, ruler of the Hebrew tribes who could order anyone killed who worked on the day he had declared the day of rest, annihilated whole cities and who was, by his own admission, "a jealous god" even to the point of insecurity, to Ishtar. Ishtar was put in charge of the third center of civilization built by the Nefilim in northern India. She was not beyond playing manipulative politics with her peers or even having one of them killed. But, in contrast to Yahweh, she instituted public sexual rituals, once a year with her foreman (king) and kept male human consorts in her palace and was the source, the institutor of a sexual "religion." Although working within the framework of the traditional interpretation, Merlin Stone says in her well researched book *When God Was A Woman*, speaking of the temple women, the *gadishtu* (holy women, sanctified women):

> Women who resided in the sacred precincts of the Divine Ancestress [Ishtar/Innana] took their lovers from among the men of the community, making love to those who came to the temple to pay honor to the Goddess. Among these people the act of sex was considered to be sacred, so holy and precious that it was enacted within the house of the Creatress . . .[26]

In Ishtar's palace or geographic precincts women were held in esteem and there is strong evidence of certain trees furnishing ritual oracular (psychedelic?) substances used in conjunction with their rites. (Sitchin states flatly that the ancient documents say that **three** types of humans were developed: men, women who were meant to bear children, women who were not meant to bear children. There may be a relationship to the topic at hand, although the **qadishtu** (also *ishtartu*) did bear children. Re-search is required here.) In Yahweh's precincts his male insecurity was mirrored in the macho-male domination of women who were considered mere property—influencing the attitudes of Western culture down to our day—and could be put to death if they were raped! There was a concerted effort on Yahweh's part to stamp out any allegiance to his female relative Ishtar. There was no love lost between them. It is clear, and reinforced by the metamorphic significance of the women's liberation movement, that we could have had a culture dominated by Ishtar's concepts rather than Yahweh's. It is not unlikely that Ishtar represented the Nefilim form of

The future will see university classes studying the psychology of the major Nefilim personalities and the formative influence on their respective areas' cultures.

emerging women's liberation in their evolutionary development at that time in their history. I submit that **this personal element is very important in understanding the traditions of any given area or culture of the world even to our times.** Further research needs to be done but I believe we can already see the root source of the gradually ritualized elements of Tantra, the sexual yoga, in the influence and practices of Ishtar as eventually partially sublimated and crystallized by Pantanjali. It is most important to note here that the Tantric tradition as propounded by the practitioners of it as a yoga is that it is a technique of consciousness expansion, a context in which, in its highest ideal form, the sexual energies are used by both partners in a highly sensitive and conscious way to create a mind-expanding and bonding psychedelic experience. It is intriguing to speculate whether this concept was received **full-blown** by chosen humans directly from the Nefilim through Ishtar. Merlin Stone's work of ten years need only be implemented or adjusted slightly in the new perspective to present us substantially with the accurate picture. **So we have before us the evidence that the Nefilim or, at least one of them, did possibly give us a ritualized technique for consciousness expansion, intelligence increase. But the practitioners of that "yoga" revered Ishtar/Innana as a humanoid Nefilim leader, an advanced Mistress of her discipline not as worshippers in a supernatural religion.**

The comparison of personality traits of the Nefilim furnishes valuable insight into the prevalent Western psychology of guilt. It is easier to overcome the dissembling false humility engendered by Yahweh's brand of subservience ethics with which we have inculcated ourselves if we realize/ recognize the source in his attitude toward humans and its source in his personality. It also helps if we recognize that the concepts we have of god-likeness, godliness, are specifically applicable, natural, only to humanoid types and are the product of a very limited situation. "Gods" from elsewhere and/or operating on other frequencies and/or other dimensions may function according to quite different relative rules, the only common denominator probably being a universal natural language based on the most fundamental physics.

The Hindu version of the Nefilim pantheon, when carefully re-scrutinized and the later popular additions and alterations sorted out, will show Ishtar dancing the role of Kali as well as the role of Shakti. But, since

**To what status is organized religion relegated when transcend-
ent experience and the occult are excised from it?**

---

the Nefilim lived so long, she is also Athena to the Greeks and this serves as
an excellent example of the unity of the pantheons of the world's cultures,
the universality of their practices and cults, a subject that has already been
partially recognized but which now becomes meaningful in a much more
significant way.

The future will see university classes studying the psychology of the
major Nefilim personalities and the formative influence on their respective
areas' culture.

These examples barely scratch the surface and I offer them with the
intention that those who are concerned with those areas of the occult will
begin to reexamine the material in the context of the new perspective.
Those already familiar with the traditional interpretations would be, most
logically, the individuals to bring to fruition the potential hidden within the
enigmatic contexts.

If, therefore, transcendent experience is a generic form of manifestation
of the prepotency of our advanced Nefilim genetic component, the leading
edge of our metamorphosis; the occult, in its valid core, packages of
advanced data, to what status is organized religion relegated when those
two components are excised from it?

The perception, in the West, of the churches as organizations holding
authority is changing on two levels. There are the obvious sociological
statistics that show the worldwide tendency to slackness of church
attendance, the refusal of members to observe moral strictures, etc. But that
is symptomatic and can alter with even a simple change to an inspiring
leader.

In the Far East, the change takes the form more of a split between an
orientation toward modern, and often technological, forms of culture and
the ancient cultural base which encompasses and is formed by the religion.
But the wealth of information and traditions contained in the ancient
scriptures preserved by the monasteries is waiting to be tapped. Nothing
need be lost; the step to transmutation is a small one in the East.

The Eastern "religions," and the Hebrew religion, since they are
historical/cultural traditions more than the religions of the West, may not
find as much difficulty making the transition. The Middle Eastern religions
and nationalities will also be motivated by a certain local territorial
proprietariness.

The deep, significant change is in the slow shift to a more relativistic mode of thought that tends to view claims of divine or unquestioned authority with a detachment and candor that is characteristic of the metamorphic shift.

Even in the Middle East, where the culture and the religion are often almost indistinguishable from one another, the growth of the moderate modern element is the most positive indicator of a slow disenfranchisement. But the Middle East is the "heartland" of our ancient beginnings, rich in that ancient history, home of those Persian astronomers who learned their trade from a tradition stemming from our education in civilization by the Nefilim, of a long heritage in science and mathematics. The potential for the Middle East to throw off its cynicism and outmoded ways to let its brilliant intellectual heritage shine once more in a position of scholarly leadership in archaeological research and integration of the new perspective is tremendous.

But the deep, significant change is in the slow shift to a more relativistic mode of thought that tends to view claims of divine or unquestioned authority with a detachment and candor that is characteristic of the metamorphic shift to a far deeper and more individual-centered orientation.

The psychological attitude and health of a member of an organization which has exhibited the openness to recognize that a reversal of its position is required and seeks to cooperate with other like organizations to lead the way will be far sounder than if his or her religious organization remained fixed.

At the time of this writing, the Pope is reiterating the fine points of the nature of angels, the Creationists, who hold for Bishop Uusher's opinion that the world and humanity were created in October of 4004 B.C. as a special case act by the Judaeo-Christian God, are suing school systems for teaching evolution, the Ayattola Komieni sends children to the war front in the name of Allah, etc. It might be argued that, in view of those signs, the prospects for the religions of the world transmuting themselves is not good. One must carefully distinguish, however, between vitality and last-gasp desperation. It will require a heroic exercise of the very virtues taught by those religions whose separate doctrines are now seen to be based on historical misinterpretations to meet the challenge of paradigm shift. If they do not the inexorable changes will occur regardless but, sadly, by erosion, neglect, attrition, decay, petrification, processes which are already visibly at work. One can only hope that the open-minded among the leaders and teachers of organized religion will sense the **continuity** that is involved in moving from their current posture to its amended extension.

The religious institutions obviously are the key entities to the removal of the theological barrier that is the single most influential factor that blocks reinterpretation of the past.

I wish to make it very clear that I do not advocate working for the elimination of institutional religion. In view of the position I hold as to the real nature of organized religious doctrine being the decadent remains and sublimation of the original master-slave relationship between the Nefilim and humans, that may seem surprising. **But the objective is to further and accelerate the planetary racial metamorphic process in all its phases to the maximum benefit of every single individual.** Ideological, social, factional, theological, philosophical competition, the Babel factor, is precisely what we do not need.

The religious institutions, obviously, are the key entities to the removal of the theological barrier that is the single most influential factor that blocks a free reinterpretation of the past. In that endeavor, undertaken by sincere leaders from within, potentially lies the intelligent transmutation of the resources, the knowledge base and the traditions of those world institutions and the greatest service to their members. The assumption of such a positive function by the organized religions would be a unique opportunity for them to heal a deep racial wound for which they are primarily responsible. The divisions between humans, manifest in theological conflict, in open ideological warfare based on religious doctrines, the persecutions and the suppressions we have seen over time could be righted. In the West, as the power of Christianity became a political as well as a religious force, theology (the study of god) split away from the approach by philosophical reason and became dominant, using as its base an unquestioning act of faith in the body of information defined as "revealed" by the Church. As soon as this radical a separation was reached the suppression and cruelty witnessed in the Inquisition and the acts of the Conquistadors was possible. The effect on the intelligent use of human reason, investigation and education up to our time has been devastating. One has only to read the daily press to notice the painful indicators as exemplified in the following typical notice:

> The memo also said discussion of seven other topics is to be restricted to material provided in the official Cobb County curriculum. These are evolution, abortion as a political or social issue, communism, religion, witchcraft, **personal inquiries and "valuing"—instructional activities designed to promote student decision-making and value selection.**
>
> Los Angeles *Times*

We must recognize and overcome the Babel factor, the long term effect of the deliberate and calculated efforts of the Nefilim to control us by the introduction of divisive factors.

The slow agony of the educational system in America has been the result of the attempt to remain Constitutionally neutral with regard to individual religious belief, the separation of Church and State. Although we trace a courageous tradition that periodically produced creative and progressive ideas it has been, so often, in spite of the prevailing outright persecution and execution and even now the cramping parameters inhibiting scientists and thinkers of great merit who have been brought up in those religious traditions. But the tendency to seek a common bond, both socially and ideologically, reinforced by the gradual recognition, in the common consciousness, of the subjective nature of truth, becomes stronger. The sense of a common history, a generic unified humanity is in the air coupled with a desire to be rid of the sickness of divisive strive. We must recognize and overcome the **Babel factor**, the long term effect of the deliberate and calculated efforts of the Nefilim to control us by the introduction of divisive factors to prevent the situation in which "nothing they propose to do will now be impossible for them" (Genesis, 11). Under the genetic imperative at the leading edge of our metamorphic process, once we have comprehended at least a little of the vision "up ahead" there is a reflexive expansion to communicate and share the knowledge. The nature of the knowledge shared by so many documented in *The Aquarian Conspiracy* by Marilyn Ferguson is of multi-dimensional generic human bonding itself. We must release this vision from the venerable but outmoded borrowed and recycled Eastern and Western theosophical contexts into the new perspective, the only context adequate enough to accommodate the pulsing groundswell of rising unitary consciousness and free it from the pressures that make it feel like a conspiracy rather than an exalted celebration. The vision of planetary racial maturity, racial enlightenment is clearly upon us; we must leave racial adolescence and accept responsibility for our own metamorphic future direction.

What is required and, hopefully, presaged in the occasional world congress of the leaders of the various major religions of the world, is a unified and concerted effort on the part of the finest minds within and without those organizations to bring about the most rapid and intelligent transmutation of the generic human tendencies that express through the organized religious medium. The Vatican Library, the Vatican Academy of Science with the great potential of its astronomical branch, the scripture

If one person has achieved the vision, the race has achieved it. If you have achieved it we—the entire race, past and present— thank you.

archives of Tibet, the Vedic tradition of India, the records of Chinese Taoism, the libraries of the monasteries throughout the world from the Benedictine to the Coptic, to the Buddhist, combined with the museums and great libraries of the world constitute a great treasure of ancient knowledge and the potential for contributing to racial enlightenment. We need to separate doctrine from history, generic human records from proprietary religious traditions. Let the monasteries, in the reverse of their conservator function in times of darkness, become the intellectual research and development centers of the completed view of human history and our unique beginning. We can no longer afford, for the survival of the race, to expend most of our metamorphic energy standing around telling each other what we should **not** be doing or thinking. We need to get the planet off hold with a multi-disciplinary intense effort that will free us to begin the integrated, unrestricted, unified, intelligence **taxing,** pleasure enhancing, religious experience producing, expanding quest for the fullness of human potential, the explanation of the nature of the cosmos and its cause, and contact with other principles of organized information processing that we can hardly imagine.

But let's maintain our perspective and our racial sense of humor. What is proposed here is, paradoxically, relatively mundane since, after all, we are going back to "pick up every stitch" of something we have already transcended; the planetary fun is yet to come.

The religions of the world need not be enervated, but transmuted in an exhilarating, compassionate, cooperative surge of planetary consciousness not to destroy but to transform and intensify in an upward movement, a Relativistic Renaissance. The root of the word "religion" is *re-ligare,* to re-bind together (L.), and the possibility of the exercise of that function through transmutation of religious institutions on a planetary scale is a challenge to which the young futants within that framework should rise. **Whatever we can comprehend we can transcend.** If one person has achieved the vision, the race has achieved it. If you have achieved it we—the entire race, past and present—thank you. We won't give you a star; maybe we'll get smart enough soon to name one after you . . .

CHAPTER 8
RACIAL ENLIGHTENMENT: ARCHAEOLOGY AS SOCIOBIOLOGY 1A

Those who are willing to handle the ambiguity of this in-between period and to anticipate the new era will be a quantum leap ahead of those who hold on to the past. The time of the parenthesis is a time of change and questioning.

John Naisbitt[26]

Don't give me no hand-me-down world...   The Guess Who

Once we have understood that, under the impetus of our advanced Nefilim genetic component, in the largest planetary picture, we are experiencing a rapid metamorphosis rather than a "normal" form of evolution; our quest for self-understanding is concentrated as transcendent experience at the leading edge of that metamorphic process; the tenacious "occult" tradition is "time-release" packets of or copying of advanced technology; the forms of organized religion are a copying and continuance of the ancient master-slave relationship as the first pottery resembled reed baskets and the first automobile resembled the wagon; the criteria by which we judge the accuracy of such information has evolved as a product of the racially naive adolescent mind-set which bound us in the fear of "the god-like in ourselves," we may begin to sort out the ramifications. This book can only be a primer that suggests the outline and scope of such a planetary endeavor.

The new paradigm throws into sharp relief the roots of a number of cultural and sociological features of contemporary human planetary society. We deal here with, as examples, traditions, customs, taboos, institutions and role models.

The general background against which to view these features is the conclusive evidence Sitchin points out that the Sumerian society possessed

...the first schools, the first bicameral congress, the first historian, the first pharmacopoeia, the first "farmer's almanac," the first cosmogony and

125

The world-wide picture is that of two groups of humans: the "in-laws," those who lived in the Nefilim centers, and the "out-laws," those living outside those centers.

cosmology, the first "Job," the first proverbs and sayings, the first literary debates, the first "Noah," the first library catalogue; and Man's first Heroic Age, his first law codes and social reforms, his first medicine, agriculture, and search for world peace and harmony.[27]

along with the protection under law of the handicapped, the poor, the widowed, the orphaned and the divorced; prohibitions against abuse of power by officials, extortion by monopoly. This tells us that all these elements that seem so modern are found in an organized, complicated society many thousands of years ago. We now know that the sudden, full blown character of that civilization was due to the decisions of the Nefilim concerning us and our adoption of their ways.

But the complete picture is of humans in the urban centers under the direct rule of the Nefilim and humans living in the wilderness areas into which they or their ancestors had been gradually expelled and where they had to literally develop a culture and a technology literally from "scratch" with, perhaps, what scraps of knowledge they retained from contact with the advanced centers. This is an important feature that is not taken into consideration by anthropologists and paleontologists because of the current common orientation: the puzzle of the hunter-gatherers and communal dwellers, the extent and sophistication of whose culture we are now only beginning to comprehend, whom we previously thought to be brutal savages and now recognize as very close to ourselves can only be fully explained in the context of Sitchin's interpretation. The cultures and traditions of the earliest humans of whom we can find a trace, and the startling worldwide similarities between those cultures, show clear signs of being an amalgam of the fragments of the civilizations (= city centers) from which they had been expelled and a sensitive attunement to the natural environment in which they lived. It was that sensitive attunement from our indigenous genetic component that was the general source of the naive, picturesque real mythology (= superstitious explanations of causes and natural phenomena resulting from ignorance) of which we have record. The world-wide picture is that of two groups of humans: the "in-laws," those who lived in the Nefilim centers, and the "out-laws," those living outside those centers.

There is a universality of certain themes and motifs running through the mythologies of all cultures, even though these are found among peoples living in different parts of the world and developing at various points in history . . .

The overrunning of the city centers by "barbarian hordes," when those Nefilim control areas weakened later in history, may well be understood as those who had been expelled finally becoming numerous and organized enough to want to claim some of the advantages they had never possessed. There is little or no difference between the tribes of France and the tribes of the Middle East; we simply see the tribes of the Middle East as somewhat more "citified" because of the context in which we view them. The entire concept of ooparts simply dissolves against this background; the abundant evidence of technology that we have interpreted as "out of place in time" was not at all out of place; much more significant is the evidence it provides that there has been a gradual **loss** over time of technology that was taught or given to us—or copied, even though not given or taught, by more precocious humans. It is easy to understand that we have the type of political, economic, social, legal and artistic forms we possess because we were given, taught them from the beginning. What is not as obvious is the nature of some of the psychological/social elements of those traditions that are so close to us that we take them as "natural."

Rhoda A. Hendricks, in *Mythologies of the World*, provides an extraordinarily concise summary of the salient characteristics of (what have traditionally been considered) the myths and legends of the world:

> There is a universality of certain themes and motifs running through the mythologies of all cultures, even though these are found among peoples living in different parts of the world and developing at various points in history . . .
>
> Most cultures had their cosmological myths, dealing with the creation and origin of the universe and mankind . . . a second creation . . . a great flood, sometimes earthquake or fire, usually brought about when the people incurred the anger of the gods, at some point after the early creation . . . new creation often due to the survival of a human pair, animals, and seeds of the new world.
>
> The dualistic principle of opposing forces and the struggle and conflict between good and evil . . . frequently represented by twins.
>
> The mother figure, or Great Mother, is found in a great number of cultures, expecially among those peoples who did not hold women in a position subordinate to men.

The focus on the exploits of heroes, many of semi-divine origin, bringing culture to their peoples has broad application to the known history of the Nefilim training us in civilization.

Mythological pairs and triads occur in almost all mythologies. The pairs were usually brother and sister, who were in many instances also husband and wife, or twins . . .

Most beliefs surrounding death show fundamental similarities in that the dead went to an afterworld . . . a number of mythologies linked death to a cycle of rebirth . . .

The theme of the exploits of heroes, performing great feats or bringing the skills of culture to their people, appears in all legends. The heroes, modeled after the gods, displayed superhuman characteristics, and many were of semidivine origin.

Foremost among the processes at work in mythology are those relating to cosmogony, the creation of the universe of the earth with its solar system, and the theory of their origin; to theogony, the origin of the gods, and their genealogy . . .

Myths were also shaped by personification, [the projection of human characteristics on nature][28]

The dualistic principle often represented by twins has a clear base in the conflict between Enlil and Enki, two brothers who were in continuing conflict concerning their assignments by the Chief of the Nefilim, their father, the power they possessed—and their conflicting opinions.

The pairs and triads involving brothers and sisters who were also husband and wife has a clear base in the Nefilim system of inheritance which seems, to us, rather arbitrary but which played a central role in their social structure. Sitchin has shown well why brothers and sisters often had children together to preserve certain status within that context. The focus on the gods and their genealogy was prevalent and important in this context.

The focus on the exploits of heroes, many of semi-divine origin (part Nefilim, part human) bringing culture to their peoples has broad application to the known history of the Nefilim training us in civilization We have yet to even begin the study of how the Nefilim or humans trained by them may have gradually contacted the tribes who had grown up in the outback from Europe to Asia to the Americas by disseminating migration; it is not surprising that the natives of Central America thought their god was returning when the fair-skinned Spaniards came ashore. The training in the

The development of designated male human kings as "foremen" clearly is the basis of the context of the "divine right of kings" concept that comes much later (1600 A.D.)

arts of civilization included a detailed description of the formation of the solar system which Sitchin has explicated well; there is little doubt that that is the source for the versions found all over the world.

Once we have understood the role of Ninhursag, the chief geneticist of the Nefilim, as literally the primary creator of humankind—her conversations concerning her scientific accomplishment in the laboratory are quite picturesque—it is a simple matter to see her as the probable source of the cult of the Great Mother, the world-wide recognition and affection found among the traces of even the earliest humans for the individual most directly responsible for our existence.

But it is the modern day form of some ancient Nefilim elements that are embedded in our culture, particularly in the West, which are of special interest here.

Consider the tradition of kingship and royalty. The prevalent form of Nefilim rulership from the beginning was of absolute, predominantly male, authority. The later development of designated male human kings as "foreman" clearly is the basis of the **context** of the "divine right of kings" concept that comes much later (1600 A.D.) but it is a generic institution established by the Nefilim throughout their known domains that does not need the rationale of the "divine right" concept.

But an important extension of the concept is in the more general notion of royalty as a privileged class. Humans reached a level above the slave state when the records begin to speak of Nefilim-human marriages, cases being known of Nefilim male and female rulers and officials having human partners and consorts. It is almost amazing that a species that had just been brought into existence should have reached a level of stability and excellence that at least some individuals could be recognized as equal with their creators that quickly. It speaks well for the closeness of the gene strains, the quality of the genetic engineering and the prepotency of the advanced Nefilim component. It is in this context that the history of the gods and demi-gods (individuals who were part Nefilim, part human by parentage) and their relationship to the queens and kings of Egypt will be best understood. When, for example, the ancient records speak of a particular queen having a god as her father, that was literally what was meant. Although the notion of a privileged class is rooted originally (although one may now buy one's title . . .) in the degree of Nefilim heritage one had

The fascination with the "life-styles of the rich and famous"; the transparent notion that to do something "like a god" is the highest compliment are all much more indicative of the "robot's" struggling to real-ize itself than we might like to think.

received rather than in simple succession from an appointed king—the Gilgamesh factor in a slightly different form again. Over time it became only a matter of being of a particular genetic line (being high-born has a significant meaning in genetic terms in the new perspective) rather than a conscious reference to the percentage of Nefilim heritage. When we witness the coronation of a new king or queen in England and deliberate intermarriage between royal families in our day to preserve lineage the phenomenon is better understood in the new perspective. The identification with and tolerance of such quaint and costly institutions may best be understood in the context of the ancient ingrained customs. The pattern of psychology so widespread throughout the world that manifests as a seeking of status, independent wealth, leisure and control of one's life and, in the highest ideal of that state, an enlightened, benevolent attitude toward those for whom one is responsible may be viewed as simply the seeking of security, as avaricious, or as a playing out of an evolutionary recapitulation of dominance mechanisms. We take almost for granted that there are or should be rulers and the ruled, royalty and commoner. It will be argued that the patterns of dominant male leadership in the animal kingdom and the higher primate societies furnish the evolutionary precedents for that phenomenon. It may be objected also that we, as part of our evolutionary development, already have those advanced "circuit's" potential in our makeup and that they are simply now gradually becoming activated in more and more of the population. But we are so close to the phenomenon and are so accustomed to ascribing the source of ubiquitous patterns of action to previous primate patterns that we do not ask obvious questions: Why should humans seek elaborate life-styles after the role models we set up? Why should we choose those role models in the first place? We do not sense the potential arbitrariness of those choices. We could perhaps just as well have adopted an individual/social ideal that gave us the security and leisure we desired that was far different in its form than the variations we consistently opt for—often at the cost of great stress. The general fascination with the "lifestyles of the rich and famous" manifest currently in a crass on-going TV program; the transparent notion that to be or do something "like a god" or "like a king" is the highest compliment one can pay are all perhaps much more indicative of the "robot's" struggling to real-ize

The tradition of royalty, of a privileged class, has remained imbedded in human societies until the present.

itself than we might like to think. I suggest that the nature of that pattern may be more a facet of our Nefilim genetic imperative **which gave us those "circuits" in the first place**. The drive to live as they lived, in that view, would be composite genetic and cultural/traditional. The tradition of royalty, of a privileged class, has remained imbedded in human societies until the present. It is significant that the self-determining thrust of the leading edge of our metamorphosis weighs heavily against that tradition. But there still remains a confusion between the concepts of the intrinsic independence and worth of the individual and the figure of heroic character, both female and male who attains status by winning it in one fashion or another. Part of that confusion is alleviated by an understanding of the role model formats that can be traced back all the way to the Nefilim masters.

From the beginning there has always been the class of officials, the scribes and the priest class who were temple servants or keepers. The multiple echelons of humans who surrounded a temple (= palace) site and contributed to its maintenance and support were carefully and thoroughly organized. The situation of a priest-official class **controlling** the temple did not arise until the Nefilim began to withdraw. We have a much more correct picture of the situation if we understand the priests as servants, as directors of the service of the physically resident god. The concept of "temple," as we have usually understood it through the popular and academic context, has been of an elaborate edifice which was the center for the worship of a god who was mythical, a sort of figure whom the popular mythos had engendered. We know now that at least some of the temples were actually inhabited either full time or part time by Nefilim individuals. The temples at Luxor or the temples of Sumer housed the Nefilim, saw their domestic day-to-day lives, their political and social ceremonies and proceedings. The menus and services and goods that were for the use and service and support of the gods were meant literally for a physical individual's food or service. The Nefilim taste in food, drink and aesthetics seem very similar to ours; not surprising: we inherited and learned from them. Leucadia, the vacation spot of the gods was probably literally just that at one time. The elaborate palaces on the islands off of Greece that were not fortified or protected were not probably because the Nefilim had total control of the world and, unless they fought among themselves, would have had no one to attack them. Around all these central sites and within the

Because of our genetic heritage we are all "royalty"; we have "instinctively" (genetically) sought that dignity and status for millennia; we have known it as ours all along.

social structures throughout the territories controlled by the Nefilim the master-slave relationship evolved into a god-ruler-people format, and eventually into a ruler-people situation. But those who were the officials, at first servants and then controlling authorities, form the background for the privileged class as we know it. In view of the emphasis on money as the common denominator in our times it is easy to lose sight of the fact that title, nobility and status as other than commoner has traditionally not been based on wealth although that status did often facilitate the accumulation of it. That tradition tends, by its nature to perpetuate the nobility-commoner dichotomy polarity.

The concept of hero originally was of a god or demi-god who could command mysterious technology, do great deeds and often is recognized as the furnisher of new inventions of great value. In the new perspective these elements take on a new meaning. Certainly the Nefilim possessed advanced technology that was awesome and totally mysterious to humans and they used it for peaceful (flight, mining, communications, etc.) as well as occasionally very destructive purposes (annihilation of cities, of their own spaceport in the Sinai, to settle disputes of leadership among themselves). The Nefilim certainly did teach us civilization and technology. It was not until they began to withdraw that the human king/hero began to come into prominence often very benevolent, sometimes despotic and cruel.

But the concept of royalty and that of hero has become confused through the gradual association of wealth as the common denominator of status. Since Western culture particularly tends to elevate the entrepreneurial achiever, the risk-taking capitalist hero tends to jet-setting privileged class "royalty" in the minds of the masses, without any relationship to personal qualities, a confusion indeed.

So the role models are distorted and tend to perpetuate subservience and class split, subjugation rather than independence. At the most fundamental level we continue to build cathedrals since we were invented to build temple-palaces. (The technology of a natural geometry taught us and embodied in the building of those edifices seems to have been the source of the Freemason tradition.) We continue to sacrifice to the sublimated concept of "God" because we were invented to supply the food and furnishings to the Nefilim in those palaces and were taught the rituals and rules concerning type, quantity and quality—in tedious detail in the case of the Hebrews' ruler, Yaheweh.

There is a theme running through human culture the source of which is not quite so evident: the cult of the sex goddess. The tradition from which it has sprung is Tantric in its roots.

But because of our genetic heritage we are all royalty; we have "instinctively" (genetically) sought that dignity and status for millennia; we have known it as ours all along; real-izing it will take some time but it is the inevitable step to the integrated status of new human. Because of that deeply felt tendency to assume our own intrinsic dignity, we have been attracted to certain role models. All are larger than life, some are transparent stereotypes and some have a deeper significance for our future direction. One serves as an excellent example of all those characteristics and also indicates the type of area which is overdue for reexamination.

There is a theme running through human culture the source of which is not quite so evident as that of the hero: the cult of the sex goddess. The tradition from which it has sprung is Tantric in its roots, has always been suppressed in the West, travelled the trade and cultural routes from India through the Middle East, found its way into Europe through the Moslem influence in Spain and the travelling Troubadours with their cult of "love," influenced the French women who had freedom, responsibility and leisure when their men went off to the Crusades, and eventually became woven into the patterns of culture that we have assimilated through our European heritage. It has finally manifested in our male-dominated and inhibited society in the decadent and distorted Hollywood sex symbol embodied in such figures as Marilyn Monroe. If the roots of the Tantric tradition began with Ishtar-Innana as seems clear then we are looking at yet another well-defined Nefilim element in our culture. We were "the black-headed ones" from the beginning. The fact that the Nefilim were tall, of light complexion and light or blond haired is in accord with the features so prominent in the latest cinematic models. The focus on the "blond goddess"—or the blond Adonis—perhaps is even partially genetic . . . simply another manifestation of the prepotency of the Nefilim gene component of human nature. The male-dominant character of our society, the roots of which we discussed in the previous chapter, is responsible for the distortion and cheapening of the image. The ancient source of the sociological phenomenon of women's liberation is clear.

There is also a dark side to our cultural traditions and practices on which the new perspective sheds light.

Consider the concept of slavery. Kings governed the people benevolently, as a rule, not in their own right but in the name of their local god and by the

Understanding the archetype of despotism is critical to our future—and a curious feature of it leads to a greater understanding of the role of the futant in our metamorphic progress.

order of that god the ancient kings often made war, conquered, subjugated populations, took slaves. The most accurate picture of the situation appears to be that they and their subjects were used as tools of war on the political chessboard of their Nefilim rulers' power struggles. There seems to be an element of almost conscious ritual in the Nefilim's political warring that was conditioned by their advanced ability to restore even life itself but that is speculation at this point. The status of humans, including kings, as about important and dispensable as chess pieces to the Nefilim is far more certain. There is record of disputes between the Nefilim, at least when humans were first invented and before the time of kingship, over who should have them or more of them since they were considered so valuable for work. But the original relationship of master-slave can be seen as the tradition from which slavery sprang, changed over time to a human-enslaving-human form. In that light the concept of slavery in those ancient times may have to be reexamined in that slavery may have been more in terms of stealing humans away from one god by another through the actions of a king and his army under orders. This is not to imply that humans could not or have not repeatedly invented the practice subsequently on their own. But the Nefilim tradition was so widespread and so fundamental that the continuance of that practice eventually by humans may be much better understood as to its roots and character in that context. The odd circumstances of the captivity and release of the Hebrews by the Egyptians is an example of both the nature of those circumstances and the authorities that actually controlled it. This background may clarify our tendencies and their sources but ultimately in no way can one excuse the inhuman and depraved traditions that have followed.

And the dark side of kingship has been the devolvement of benevolent rulership—the dominant characteristic of the original kings—into the despotic and cruel subjugation of fellow humans at various times throughout subsequent history. In the final analysis we are surely looking at a blend of the basic anthropoid element of male dominance combined with a decadent copying of the Nefilim brand of master-slave control. Understanding the archetype of despotism is critical to our future—and a curious feature of it leads to a greater understanding of the role of the futant in our metamorphic progress.

The blond teutonic superman figure is an uncanny irruption of the preponent Nefilim genetic component in the collective unconscious little different from the blond sex goddess archetype.

It is within this context that Timothy Leary's evaluation of the futant gone awry makes immanent sense; he characterizes Adolph Hitler as both

> a male-macho-militaristic-murderer [and] . . . a futant whose brain had been activated five stages ahead of his hive . . . a 21st century brain imprinted by the militaristic German-hive and conditioned by the lower-class middle-European nastiness yet, . . . from a compassionate non-partisan post-terrestrial perspective . . . the most effective futant explorer the planet Earth had produced up to his confused epoch.[30]

Even after we have recognized the future elements in the Nazi ethos: first space rockets, use of electronic communication, incorporation of Buddhist, Tibetan, Sufi knowledge as part of their political philosophy, the use of self-actualizing drugs, peyote, hashish, cocaine and amphetamines (invented by German chemists) the one dominant feature that stands out is the Aryan Super-Race myth. I submit that the "haunting attraction" of the Blond Teutonic superman figure is an uncanny irruption of the prepotent Nefilim genetic component in the collective unconscious little different from the Blond Sex Goddess archetype.

But, on the positive side, there is a point crucial to our exploration of a new sociobiology contained here regarding the subject of futants in general: once we have recognized the nature of the futant genetic potential we should immediately realize that without sufficient constructive context within to operate the futant can—witness Adolph who, as Wilson has pointed out, took Nietzsche's *description* of the horrors of the status quo as a *prescription*—go disastrously awry. On the one hand, as Leary points out,

> The Megolomaniac Dictator obviously plays a vital and necessary role in human evolution If he didn't, rest assured he would not pop up in every successful-expansionist gene-pool in human history.[31]

But Leary—quite obviously the most advanced futant psychologist on the planet—also states the converse:

> Self-confident brains like Hitler's will become the Dom-Species (dominant, prevalent) in a few decades . . . will not be used to fabricate weird primitive genocidal cults; but will perform **routine tasks of reality creation** . . .[32]

There is no longer need for the eruptive archetypal bursts from the collective unconscious to force us blindly on to the next plateau.

If Hitler represents the epitome of the dark side, the new perspective furnishes the illuminated historical context against which the future oriented positive *Exo-psychology* of Leary can be fully appreciated, the real significance of Jung's archetypes can be understood, and the role of the futant integrated. There is no longer a need for the extreme aberrations of human psychology as exemplified by the Megolomaniac Dictator in the unfolding of our racial metamorphosis if we will acknowledge ourselves for what we are; there is no longer need for the eruptive archetypal bursts from the collective unconscious to force us blindly on to the next plateau.

The futant groping with some trepidation into the future, more often than not misunderstood and isolated from mainstream peers and sometimes wracked from early childhood by parentally or socially repressed drives that he/she may not understand, should be a phenomenon of the past. Only the most erudite, experienced and disciplined futants are able to sustain the burden of isolation, misunderstanding and the Semmelweis reflex. The Semmelweis Reflex [as defined by Leary]:

> Mob behavior found among primates and larval hominids on undeveloped planets, in which a discovery of important scientific fact is punished rather than rewarded. Named after Dr. Ignaz Semmelweis, . . . physician who discovered the cause of puerperal fever, a now-obsolete disease which, in Semmelweis's primitive era, yearly killed a vast number of women in childbirth. Semmelweis was fired from his hospital, expelled from his medical society, denounced and ridiculed widely, reduced to abject poverty and finally died in a madhouse . . . [33]

The genuine futant should be integrated into our society and reinforced as routinely as the IBM corporation supports its Research Fellows.

In previous chapters we have dealt with the major broad issues. These more specific examples are intended to indicate the depth, ubiquity, and obviousness of the elements from our true past that continue to form, color and influence us in our daily lives. They are intended to indicate to the specialist in every field the extent to which sociological as well as scientific, psychological and artistic, re-examination of our entire planetary society is required.

We are moved by a genetic imperative at the leading edge of our metamorphosis that prompts our action, seeking and analysis more, perhaps, than we are comfortable yet with admitting.

There are a myriad of relatively trivial indicators that are almost amusingly apparent: the significance of the sacred legend of an Eskimo tribe which says that the original members of their group arrived there in prehistoric times "on the wings of an iron bird" (how far into the outback did they systematically dump us!?); the beehive shaped hat on some Buddha statues and the tiara, the three tiered conical crown worn by the Pope of Rome (after a traditional Persian jeweled crown) both of which symbolize divinity and which mimic the Nefilim headdress (probably associated with a communications device) and the horned headdress of the Norsemen almost identical to another Nefilim type; our taken-for-granted orientation to gold; our orientation to "up" as the goal, the good, as expressed in our rocketry, our space exploration, our aspirations—and even how we describe our sense of well-being, ie., "I feel really 'up' today"; our mode of elaborate dress and use of jewels for formal, "important occasion" dress; the real basis for and structure of the caste system in India, etc.

But it is the sweeping ramifications rather than the trivial symptoms that are most important, however, when we survey the state of planetary society. Two features stand out clearly in the overview: the planet is "on hold" but there are a number of currents of thought, vectors of analysis expressing the impulses from the collective consciousness, taking the bearings and attempting to point the direction toward the "new era."

If is not difficult to see that the planet is not only on "hold" because we have reached a point at which we are recycling traditions, religious beliefs, educational patterns, political systems, philosophies and scientific attitudes that are clearly and simply not in keeping with the fullness of the vision of human potential we all privately know and desire. It is more difficult to see the target of the vectors however because there is a certain amount of recycling involved in their expression, their vision only extends to the next statistically comfortable step or is confined to only a few dimensions, or critical pieces of information are lacking to create the "critical-mass" required for the truly grand vision. But their potential is tremendous and all contribute, all mutually reinforce, whether it be negatively or positively— although the latter is a lot more comfortable and fun—we are all of one field of consciousness, moved by a genetic imperative at the leading edge of our

**Consider the powerful cluster of glowing vectors on our
intellectual radar, the signs we keep leaving for ourselves all
generated by the same generic impulse at the leading edge
of our probing.**

metamorphosis that prompts us collectively and individually and
determines our action, seeking and analysis more, perhaps, than we
are comfortable yet with admitting. (Richard Dawkins in *The Selfish
Gene*[34] has given us a wry description of how he sees the genes use us
as vehicles through which to perpetuate their kind. If we put his thesis
in the new perspective we can perhaps best understand the pressures
he—we—feel from the genetic base in terms of the accelerating
impetus of our metamorphosis due to the bicameral nature of our
genetic base although the transcendence of his keen intellect and wry
wit would almost paradoxically belie the determinism he is
describing.)

Consider the powerful cluster of glowing vectors on our intellectual
radar, the indicators we have created to tell ourselves where to look
and what to look for, the signs we keep leaving **ahead** of ourselves all
generated by the same inexorable generic impulse at the leading edge
of our probing.

John Naisbitt in *Megatrends* has given us a lucid picture of the
immediate future as we move from the industrial age to the
information age through the "time of the parenthesis" as has Alvin
Toffler in *The Third Wave*[35] a more sociologically somber mode. Daniel
Boorstin in *The Discoverers*[36] has filled in the profiles of the sometimes
timorous, sometimes intrepid futant personalities who have been the
focal metamorphic operators over the ages. We are indebted to them
for the scholarly and expert delineation of details of symptoms
whether it be on a clinically economic basis, a courageous dealing with
the possible dangers of the processes, or a benevolent expose of
contributions and both the strong and weak characteristics of
sometimes too human explorers. Though perhaps too unidimensional
their contributions in their fields of expertise do elucidate the clear
direction and detail and character of our common "upward" drive in
those areas toward the recognition of the intrinsic worth, freedom and
self-determination of the individual in terms of wealth, leisure, self-
expression. We translate those terms easily into the more general
concept of reality controller, self-determining reality creator.

Teilhard de Chardin's work,[37] Lawrence Blair in *Rhythms of Vision*,[38]
Marilyn Ferguson in *The Aquarian Conspiracy* enlarge the view, add a
dimension and express the vectors in terms of a planetary connection

We would never come together as a race, relax the barriers of nation, religion, culture, custom, philosophy unless and until we can see that we were partially correct.

between all men, peace and the alleviation of want, the elimination of the "optical illusion" Einstein said made us see ourselves as separate, the growing sense of a communicatory field of consciousness, the "upward" movement toward a transcendent unification, the change to more adequate systems. Marilyn's words are so poignantly close to the point: if we have "followed the wrong god home" and feel a need to break with our history it is indicative of reaching the critical-mass point where we recognize that we are each the more than metaphorical "god" we should be following and that happily the only history we have to break with is that interpretation that has kept us so effectively separated from our true past. We are indebted to them for their abilities to crystallize such lucid concepts out of the currents of inchoate sentiment. They are representatives of the "yeast of change," the real "free thinkers" pointing to an "imminent world transformation." To complete the urgent vision they have begun we need only repair the real break with our history and provide indication of the startling genetic nature of our creation to break the barrier and see that we are home already.

Emerging from the network of expanding consciousness we find the work of Wheeler, Zukave, Capra, Wolf, Young, Wilber, Loye, Sheldrake and Briggs and Peat and Sarfatti along with many others probing the subtle reaches of the mind field, suggesting the integration of the concepts of the most advanced quantum physics with the concepts of the ancient teachings from the East, unlimbering the ancient vocabularies and lore of the occult to make the enigmas of the quantum level the tools of expression for our transcendent experience, examining our potential communications through the quantum potential, hinting at scientifically verifiable multidimensional consciousness. They supply vectors at a point of convergence that is unique and pivotal in our progress. They point, each in their own way, to the focal point of the expansion of the mind of the new humanity. We need only add the historical clarity of the new perspective to show how "godlike" that new mentality turns out to be.

When all the explorers have shown their slides, Sitchin's thesis is the lights going on in the auditorium. And Robert Anton Wilson (*Prometheus Rising*)[39] delivers the explanatory lecture, an erudite, masterful "vector analysis," a last minute briefing on what's to come.

We all have the inchoate vision inside us, in our genes, indeed are all the vision itself.

We are at far more of a "turning point" than even the one Capra envisions; in possession of far more of a "web of reinforcement" than Baines could hope for; the morphogenetic field potential is far higher than Sheldrake predicts; the groundswell documented by Ferguson is about to become a tsunami, with a capability to take the planet off hold and close the "vision gap" in a way that is perhaps more comprehensive than conceived by Barbara Marx Hubbard. We would never come together as a race, relax the barriers of nation, religion, culture, custom, philosophy unless and until we can all see that we were partially correct and that the vision which finally unites us is what we expected all along, **subsumes all worldviews, all cultures, all religions, all contexts.** We all have the inchoate vision inside us, in our genes, indeed are all the vision itself. We do not need to discover that vision; we need only to acknowledge it, acknowledge ourselves, seize our true history.

The clear message from genetic center: gratefully acknowledge the past, be free of parental conditioning, accept racial adulthood, claim your true inheritance, create your future.

The final question always is: Where do we go from here? What model what outline, map do we have that is adequate to incorporate the vision and allow us to by a course into the future? If we heed the genetic message, we will need a genetic map.

Timothy Leary's *Info-Psychology* (New Falcon Publications, 1993) is subtitled *A Manual On The Use Of The Human Nervous System According To The Instructions Of The Manufacturers…*! It is

> deliberately eclectic and translational—linking the religious-occult to the scientific; the mundane to the futique; the legends of the past to the data of the present.

It details, far past the bio-survival "circuits,"

> …three post-larval levels of contelligence which are defined by anatomical structure…:
> **Neurosomatic Contelligence:** body reality. The reception, integration and transmission of sensory-somatic signals.
> **Neurophysical Contelligence** located in the cerebral cortex mediating the reality of the brain, electromagnetic signals.

The new planetary paradigm is one of ultimate ecology in that not only nothing need be lost but everything may be saved and contribute.

Neurogenetic Contelligence: transceiving DNA signals via RNA.

We need only add the modifier "interrupted" to the word evolution and read this message—that stretches our current vision into the future far enough to create a sort of intellectual parallax—against the background of our "new history" to provide it the integrated context it deserves. Rather than outline Leary's work completely I simply make the flat statement: there is, at this point in time, no other more elegant, comprehensive, advanced message from the DNA around. The model presented in *Exopsychology* and the more recent *Game of Life* will be an adequate **model** for some time to come. The message: Imprint the DNA; tune in to the most fundamental set of directions we know from the miniaturized transceiver intelligence that builds us—and then playfully transcend them, summed up in the acronym SMI²LE for Space Migration, Intelligence increase, Life Extension, a precise statement of the genetic imperative driving us at the leading edge of our accelerating metamorphosis—and, not surprisingly, a precise description of the "gods" that truth, the real humility, requires us to acknowledge that we are. In light of the overwhelming evidence it would be arrogant **not** to.

Tim Leary's personal adventure is a significant vector in itself. The Semmelweis Reflex put him through twenty-five jails as virtually a political prisoner for insisting that the individual has the inviolable right to manipulate, explore, expand, control Hir neurological system/brain/mind and espousing psychedelic chemicals as the best tool so far to achieve that end, the exploration of the metamorphic leading edge. As a result his intelligence and sense of humor is keener than ever and the refinement of the genetic message he transmits ever clearer. This is eloquent testimony to the efficacy of the principles he follows, and the refined level of neuropolitical "aikido" against the Semmelweis Reflex the range of his futant vision allows him to exercise.

The new planetary paradigm is one of ultimate ecology in that not only nothing need be lost but everything may be saved and contribute. It is at once collective in that it is of generic, unified planetary humanity yet based on the absolute freedom of self-determination. It is completely comprehensive in time because it finally reconciles and integrates our past with our present

The new paradigm integrates our fragmented sociobiology by integrating our criteria, our science, our politics, our psychology and our transcendental experience.

and points to the future. Having removed the spell of the lesser gods we have mistakenly followed home we will see as alien only those who would erect or maintain the truly mythic great walls, the barriers that divide. It provides a perspective that prevents entrapment by worldviews that must prohibit or restrict to survive, allowing unconditional participation in a process of discovery at the leading edge of our metamorphic transcendence that is more than satisfactory now that it is not proprietary or parts of it *a priori* taboo. It returns our minds to us relieved of the impossible and stultifying burden of knowing everything, the absolutely ultimate Cause of the universe and therefore truly self-confident (the opposite of arrogant), shameless (unhampered by arbitrary taboos and oriented to complete disclosure), free (unconditionally responsible for oneself, uncoerced to accept some "higher" authority) and enables us to participate playfully and cooperatively in the sanity of the unlimited process of transcendent intelligence increase. The new paradigm integrates our fragmented sociobiology by integrating our criteria, our science, our politics, our psychology and our transcendental experience. It frees our science to integrate the information we may be able to retrieve from the past and is the context in which the "occult" disciplines will rediscover their identity. It provides the context within which we can break the patterns of outmoded, recycled explanations, frustrated iconoclasm, cramping alienation in a sort of reunion in which those who, in their newly acquired maturity, laugh together about their adolescent rivalries.

The single purpose of this work has been to go back to make clear the ramifications of the archaeological integration. It remains for the experts in their fields to contemplate, explore, integrate, explicate, and innovate in the new dimension of generic humanity as we break the larval shell of primitive concepts hardened through the ages, dry the wings of our own responsibility and independence—aware that, in a significant expansion of our sociobiology, the mating flight will be off-planet.

EPILOGUE

We shall not cease from exploration
And the end of all our exploring
Will be to arrive where we started
And know the place for the first time.

T.S. Eliot

How can I say these things in the face of the evening news . . .

Because, in the face of an almost paralyzing sense of the subjective and sollipsistic nature of our proofs and convictions and the relativity of our thinking, I have seen enough pattern in the context to have made a very calculated bet in formulating the model put forth here and I do not bet easily. This with a full appreciation of the fact that the adequacy of the model will be valid only for a short time and that the model is still another anthropoid projection that I sincerely hope will embarrass me in the near future.

Because scientists do not want to refuse to look at certain phenomena; religionists do not want to be separatist, and oppressive; philosophers do not want to argue; theologians do not want to disagree; the vast majority of humans do not want to see the other as the enemy—they only **think they have to** because of conditioning; must according to inculcated principles; feel they have no choice because that is the rule of the game.

Because the mind of the ordinary human is more than capable of discerning partial or partisan or incorrect explanations than generally given credit for; the keen perception of incomplete or inaccurate information and the concomitant hesitation may not be articulated but its result is certain.

Because we are all rather strange even to ourselves, as neophyte adults are, even a bit funny, making overconfident position statements at the same time we are looking out of the corner of our eye to see if we might be making fools of ourselves. It has been our cultural short-sightedness, our fears, our divisiveness, ultimately our collective lack of planetary racial maturity—but it has been ours, the only game around and it is ours to transmute. The overwhelming response from those with whom I have

143

discussed the subject has been a deep affirmation from their subjective conviction that it's substantially correct. I take this as a signal from genetic central. If there is sufficient, comprehensive ground to accept a new view we all will with relief.

Because we all know in our most private thoughts that we can't go off into space looking for contact with other races until we know who and what we are. We can't seek mature contact and association—much less union—with alien species until we have matured past our racial adolescence, and this is the only model that makes the comprehensive "sense" to integrate our past in filling out our maturity.

Because quite certainly we are philotropic, wisdom-seeking and possessed of a hunger for new dimensions and self-knowledge.

Because whatever we can comprehend we can transcend.

Because when DNA speaks, **everybody** listens.

FOOTNOTES

1.   T.B. Pawlicki, *How to Build a Flying Saucer: And Other Proposals In Speculative Engineering*, (Englewood Cliffs, NJ: Prentice Hall, 1981), p. 141.

2.   C.W. Ceram, *Gods, Graves, and Scholars*, (New York: Alfred A. Knopf, 1967)

3.   Speiser, E.A., Ancient Mesopotamia, (pages 35-76 in Dentan, R.C. (editor), *The Idea of History in the Ancient Near East*, American Oriental Series 38, (New Haven: Yale University Press and Oxford University Press, London, 1855), pp. 49-50.

4.   R.A. Shotwell, *An Introduction To The History of History*, (New York, Columbia University Press, 1923), p. 13.

5.   Erasmus Darwin, *Zoonomia, or the Laws of Organic Life*, reprint of 2 vols. 1796 (New York, AMS Press).

6.   Charles Darwin, *The Origin of Species*, (London, John Murray, 1859).

7.   Charles Darwin, *The Descent Of Man*, (London, John Murray, 1871, 2 vols.)

8.   Stephen Jay Gould, *Ever Since Darwin*, (New York, W.W. Norton, 1977).

9.   Rene Noorbergen, *Secrets Of The Lost Races*, (New York, Barnes and Noble, 1977), pp. 2-3.

10.   Zecharia Sitchin, (The Earth Chronicle Series), The *Twelfth Planet*, (New York, Stein and Day, 1976): *The Stairway to Heaven*, (New York, Avon, 1980): *The Wars of Gods and Men*, (New York, Avon, 1985).

11.   Gould, op.cit. p. 159.

12.   Randolfo Rafael Pozos, *The Face On Mars*, (Chicago, Chicago Review Press, 1986).

13.   Gordon Childe, *Prehistoric Migrations in Europe*, (Cambridge, MA: Harvard University Press, 1950).

14.   Richard Leakey, *The Making Of Mankind*, (New York, E.P. Dutton, 1981), pp. 30-31.

15.   (David Pilbeam, Ph.D., "The Descent of Hominoids and Hominids," *Scientific American*, March 1984, p. 96.

16.   Edward O. Wilson, *Sociobiology*, The abridged edition, (Cambridge, MA and London, England, The Belknap Press of Harvard University Press, 1980), p. 272.

17.   Abraham H. Maslow: reference lost

18.   Timothy Leary, *Exo-Psychology*, (Sedona, AZ, Falcon Press, 1987), p. 32.

19.   Sidney Brett, (*Psychology, Ancient and Modern*), (New York, Coopers Square, 1963)

20.   Gerald Heard, *The Five Ages of Man* (New York, Julian Press, 1962)

21.   Timothy Leary, op.cit. p. 10-11

22.   Edward De Bono, (Interview in *Omni*, March 1985), p. 118.

23.   Marilyn Ferguson, *The Aquarian Conspiracy*, (Los Angeles, Tarcher, 1980), p. 408.

24.   Stan Tenen, *Torus*, vol. 1, #5, 1985; #2/3 1983.

25.   Dennis J. and Terence McKenna, *The Invisible Landscape*, (New York, Seabury Press, 1975)

26.   Merlin Stone, *When God Was A Woman*, (San Diego, New York, London, Harcourt Brace Jovanovich, A Harvest/HBJ Book, 1976), p. 154.

27.   John Naisbitt, *Megatrends*, (New York, Warner Books, 1984), p. 279.

28.   Zecharia Sitchin, *The Twelfth Planet*, ibid., p. 46.

29.   Rhoda A. Hendricks, *Mythologies of the World*, (New York, McGraw Hill, 1979), pp. xii-xiii.

30.   Timothy Leary, *The Game of Life*, (Sedona, AZ, Falcon Press, 1987) 34.

31.   ————, *ibid.*, p. 254.

32. ————, *ibid.*, p. 254.

33. ————, ibid., p. 43.

34. Richard Dawkins, *The Selfish Gene,* (New York, The Oxford University Press, 1976).

35. Alvin Toffler, *The Third Wave*, (New York, Bantam Books, 1982).

36. Daniel J. Boorstin, *The Discoverers*, (New York, Vintage, Random House, 1985).

37. Pierre Teilhard de Chardin, see, as representative work: *The Future of Man*, (New York, Harper and Row, 1959).

38. Lawrence Blair, *Rhythms of Vision*, (New York, Shocken Books, 1976).

39. Robert Anton Wilson, *Prometheus Rising*, (Sedona, AZ, Falcon Press, 1983).

RETROSPECTIVE

This third printing allows me an opportunity, rare to an author, to offer the reader a retrospective on *Breaking the Godspell* and significant events, pertinent to its thesis, that have occurred subsequent to its first printing in 1987.

Time has shown me that which I subjectively consider the factual content of the book to be fundamentally correct, perhaps even stronger, reinforced by information coming to light all the time. I can say, unequivocally, that there is nothing in the book that I would change—at least to date—except, perhaps, some of the sentence structures for ease of reading. If one has contemplated and expressed a powerful new thesis for some time, putting it on paper can be easy and the expression comfortable. It was a curious thing to me, even then, that, because the import of the information that was coming in such a rush, was so powerful and novel, the expression reflected my state of mind. I have been chided by some readers for the convolutions of thought but not for the content.

To date, I have done one hundred and eleven radio talk show telephone interviews all over the United States, several TV interviews and a number of lectures and presentations. I was initially amazed, frankly, that, even in the Bible Belt, I have received roughly eight-five percent positive reception and feedback from listener call-ins, and a wide variety of audiences. But a pattern emerged: the overwhelmingly typical response was "I have been thinking about these things all my life, always thought that there had to be some more comprehensive explanation, and your book seems to finally say it right." I have come to have a deep respect for the keen perception, sensitivity and sheer depth of thought of the "ordinary" citizen. It is, paradoxically, the academic community that lags behind, mired in a turfish protectionism.

Since December of 1991 I have been the host of a private electronic conference on the WELL bulletin board focused on a critical discussion of my work and the work of Zecharia Sitchin. Fortunately the ten members of the conference, all of very high and independent intellectual caliber, do not always agree and the arguments and discussion have ranged from humorous to hot. I am grateful to my electronic colleagues for the criticism and constructive information and reinforcement that I have received from them. Even after two years the conference is productive and the intensity of the discussions indicative of the importance of the topic.

The multiple vectors of information reinforcing the new paradigm are converging faster and more intensely. Zecharia Sitchin has published a great deal more excellent archaeological and linguistic material; the mitochondrial DNA "search for Eve" work has pointed to the same spot on the African map for the first human where the Nefilim genetic laboratory is described in the old records. The gold mining engineers of Africa now go looking for the traces of the old Nefilim mines rather than start geologically from scratch and some mines have been dated to 65,000 years, possibly 100,000 years old. Stringer's "out of Africa" anthropological theory, accounting for the rise of modern humans, tallies with the old records and the discovery of Neanderthal man contemporary with modern humans and possibly arising after modern humans had come on the scene, correlates with the ancient records and has blown previous theory out of the water. The work of Maurice Chatelain, former head of the Apollo missions communications, Carl Munck, retired Air Force, David Hatcher Childress and others has brought to our attention a global grid system based on a precise measurement of the circumpolar circumference of the earth that existed in ancient times. Torun, Carlotto, Hoagland and others have shown that the alleged "artificial constructions" on Mars manifest relationships based on a sophisticated spherically enclosed tetrahedral geometry that seems to be analogous to the grid system on Earth. Sitchin had published the archaeological evidence for the Nefilim presence on Mars and Earth a number of years ago and this new evidence fills in some of the details of that connection. Shoch and West have presented geological evidence for the age of the Sphinx being at least 9000 years old. Joseph Davidovits, the French chemist inventor of geopolymeric cement, has analyzed the material of the building blocks of the Giza Pyramid and shown that they were cast in place of a sophisticated geopolymeric cement. Both of these recent findings are strong evidence for the claim made in the ancient records that the Nefilim built both the Giza pyramid complex and the Sphinx.

As a generalist who must understand and consider the work of all the experts, it is already clear to me that all these vectors reinforce the new paradigm. Furthermore, I believe that the evidence supports my theory that the Nefilim, many thousands of years ago had reached a point where they had developed a unified field theory, a theory of everything, based on the meta-metaphor of self-reference. This theory, which I elaborate in my next book, God Games, has a major advantage in that it explains not only the physical realm but our intelligence in terms of our self-referential consciousness. I believe that the spherical/tetrahedral geometry embodied in the Giza Pyramid and the world grid of which it is a cornerstone and its analog as found on Mars is a special application of the Nefilim unified field theory physics. Interestingly, the same kind of approach and topology has been rediscovered by Stan Tenen of the Meru Foundation as the basis of the self-referential system that forms the Hebrew alphabet characters and the alphabets of a number of other ancient languages. I suggest that this is another special application of the Nefilim approach to the universe in linguistics.

Obviously there has been a great deal of development in the general area of the new paradigm. But my focus has always been on the leading edge ramifications of our being a genetically engineered and subservient species until the Nefilim phased off the Earth. It is the development of the significance of our restored history and the radical freedom it allows us that I am working on in God Games.

The new synthesis subsumes the groundswell rising to a new politic, enlightened eco-economics, re-hashed Eastern or Western mysticism, a third culture, spiritualized psychology, cerebral turning points, religion as we have ever conceived it, and the old New Age. It's time to turn the Aquarian conspiracy into a celebration. The word from station DNA is that these "gods" wear designer genes.

What to do after you get genetically enlightened and have broken the godspell, the effect of the ancient, subservient, looking-to-the-sky-for-daddy-to-return, master-slave attitude, the deepest dye in the fabrics of Eastern and Western culture? Physical immortality, possessed by the Nefilim probably through genetic engineering and withheld from humans, is seen as a collective preoccupation and the dominant characteristic of the dawning new phase of our racial maturation. The characteristics that mark the new human are an unassailable personal integrity, relativistic epistemology, profound compassion, robust depth of informational data, understanding of the universe in terms of a full unified field, broad-spectrum competence, transcendental competition, facility in dimensional shifting, preference for dyadic operation, a profound ability to enjoy, to play the games most enjoyable and satisfying to generic "gods", an expanded capacity to literally have great fun creating new realities, with the primary focus on the multidimensional—and getting ready to step confidently into stellar society. The totems and taboos of our racial adolescence dispelled, Prometheus can get off his rock and reach genetic satori; Job can get off his dung heap and complete his EST training; Buddha can open his eyes and reach genetic enlightenment.

Neil Freer
La Costa, California
November 9, 1993

***God Games: What Do You Do Forever?* by Neil Freer**. "Then came Neil Freer [who] undertook a different kind of mind-boggling task. If all that I had concluded was true, he said, what does it all mean, not to the human race and the planet in general—what does it mean to the individuals, to each one of us? He titles his new book God Games. But, if all the above is the Truth, it is not a game." Zecharia Sitchin (from the Introduction). This new book by Neil Freer, author of *Breaking the Godspell*, outlines the human evolutionary scenario far into the future. Freer describes what's in store for us as our dawning genetic enlightenment reveals the new human and the racial maturity of a new planetary civilization on the horizon. We all can contribute to our future as we evolve from a slave  species to far beyond what we could previously even imagine. The godspell broken, we new humans will create our own realities and play our own "god games." According to Freer, once we understand our true genetic history we will eventually move beyond the gods, religion, linear consciousness and even death. It is quite possible that great thinkers in the future will look back on this book as being the one which opened the door to our full evolutionary potential and a new paradigm. Neil Freer is a brilliant philosopher, focused on the freedom of the individual and what it means to be truly human. This book will make you think in new and different ways. Accept the challenge of God Games and you will be greatly rewarded. **ISBN 1-885395-39-6 • 312 pages • 6 x 9 • trade paper • $19.95**

***Of Heaven and Earth: Essays Presented at the First Sitchin Studies Day*, edited by Zecharia Sitchin**. Zecharia Sitchin's previous books have sold millions around the world. This book, first published in 1996, contains further information on his incredible theories about the origins of mankind and the intervention by intelligences beyond the Earth. Sitchin, in previous works, offers the most scholarly and convincing approach to the ancient astronaut theory you will most certainly ever find. This book offers the complete transcript of the first Sitchin Studies Day, held in Denver, Colorado on Oct. 6, 1996. Zecharia Sitchin's keynote address opens the book, followed by six other prominent speakers whose work has been influenced by Sitchin. The other contributors to the book include two university professors, a clergyman, a UFO expert, a philosopher, and a novelist—who joined Zecharia Sitchin in Denver, Colorado, to describe how his findings and conclusions have affected what they teach and preach. They all seem to agree that the myths of ancient peoples were actual events as opposed to being figments of imaginations. Another point of agreement is in Sitchin's work being the early part of a new paradigm—one that is already beginning to shake the very foundations of religion, archaeology and our society in general. **ISBN 1-885395-17-5 • 164 pages • 5 1/2 x 8 1/2 • trade paper • illustrated • $14.95**

***Enuma Elish: The Seven Tablets of Creation (in two volumes)*, by L. W. King**. Subtitled: The Babylonian and Assyrian Legends Concerning the Creation of the World and of Mankind. The *Enuma Elish* is one of the oldest stories known to mankind. It is a story first written down by the ancient Sumerians thousands of years ago. As a one-time assistant in the Department of Egyptian and Assyrian Antiquities at the British Museum, L. W. King provides us with a qualified translation of the tablets that were originally written in cuneiform script. The *Enuma Elish* is receiving renewed interest from modern researchers delving into the origins of mankind, the earth, and the solar system. Over the centuries a copy ended up in the library at Nineveh in the 7th century BC, and was uncovered by archaeologists in the late 1800s. Written in  cuneiform text and preserved on seven clay tablets, the entire story was called *The Seven Tablets of Creation*. After being translated the story revealed how the planets became aligned, how a cosmic catastrophe affected the earth, how mankind came upon the scene, and how the "gods" played a role in all of it. *The Seven Tablets of Creation* have had many profound implications since they were first discovered and published. They predate many parts of the Book of Genesis as well as other worldwide creation myths. Volume One includes this epic poem's English translation. It also includes information on parallels in Hebrew literature, the date and origin of the Babylonian creation legends, and more. **Vol 1: ISBN 1-58509-041-7 • 236 pages • 6 x 9 • trade paper • illustrated • $18.95. Vol 2: ISBN 1-58509-042-5 • 260 pages • 6 x 9 • trade paper • illustrated • $19.95**

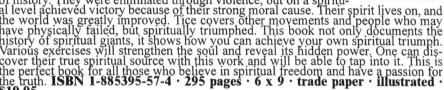

Triumph of the Human Spirit: The Greatest Achievements of the Human Soul and How Its Power Can Change Your Life, by Paul Tice. A triumph of the human spirit happens when we know we are right about something, put our heart into achieving its goal, and then succeed. There is no better feeling. People throughout history have triumphed while fighting for the highest ideal of all -- spiritual truth. Tice brings you back to relive and explore history's most incredible spiritual moments, bringing you into the lives of visionaries and great leaders who were in touch with their souls and followed their hearts. They explored God in their own way, exposed corruption and false teachings, or freed themselves and others from suppression. People like Gandhi, Joan of Arc, and Dr. King expressed exactly what they believed and changed the entire course of history. They were eliminated through violence, but on a spiritual level achieved victory because of their strong moral cause. Their spirit lives on, and the world was greatly improved. Tice covers other movements and people who may have physically failed, but spiritually triumphed. This book not only documents the history of spiritual giants, it shows how you can achieve your own spiritual triumph. Various exercises will strengthen the soul and reveal its hidden power. One can discover their true spiritual source with this work and will be able to tap into it. This is the perfect book for all those who believe in spiritual freedom and have a passion for the truth. **ISBN 1-885395-57-4 · 295 pages · 6 x 9 · trade paper · illustrated · $19.95**

Mysteries Explored: The Search for Human Origins, UFOs, and Religious Beginnings, **by Jack Barranger and Paul Tice**. Jack Barranger and Paul Tice are two authors who have combined forces in an overall investigation into human origins, religion, mythology, UFOs, and other unexplained phenomena. In the first chapter, "The Legacy of Zecharia Sitchin", Barranger covers the importance of Sitchin's *Earth Chronicles* books, which is creating a revolution in the way we look at our past. In "The First Dragon" chapter, Tice examines the earliest known story containing dragons, coming from Sumerian/Babylonian mythology. In "Past Shock", Barranger suggests that events which happened thousands of years ago very strongly impact humanity today. In "UFOs: From Earth or Outer Space?" Tice explores the evidence for aliens being from other earthly dimensions as opposed to having an extraterrestrial origin. "Is Religion Harmful?" looks at the origins of religion and why the entire idea may no longer be working for us, while "A Call to Heresy" shows how Jesus and the Buddha were considered heretics in their day, and how we have reached a critical point in our present spiritual development that requires another such leap. Aside from these chapters, the book also contains a number of outrageous (but discontinued) newsletters, including: Promethean Fire, Pleiadian Poop, and Intrusions. **ISBN 1-58509-101-4 · 104 pages · 6 x 9 · trade paper · $12.95**

Past Shock: The Origin of Religion and Its Impact on the Human Soul, **by Jack Barranger.** Twenty years ago, Alvin Toffler coined the term "future shock" — a syndrome in which people are overwhelmed by the future. *Past Shock* suggests that events that happened thousands of years ago very strongly impact humanity today. Technologically advanced beings created us as a slave race and in the process spiritually raped us. This book reveals the real reasons why religion was created, what organized religion won't tell you, the reality of the "slave chip" programming we all have to deal with, why we had to be created over and over again, what really happened in the Garden of Eden, what the Tower of Babel was and the reason why we were stopped from building it, how we were conditioned to remain spiritually ignorant, and much more. Jack exposes what he calls the "pretender gods,"

advanced beings who were not divine, but had advanced knowledge of scientific principles which included genetic engineering. Our advanced science of today has unraveled their secrets, and people like Barranger have the knowledge and courage to expose exactly how we were manipulated. Learn about our past conditioning, and how to overcome the "slave chip" mentality to begin living life as it was meant to be, as a spiritually fulfilled being. **ISBN 1-885395-08-6 · 126 pages · 6 x 9 · trade paper · illustrated · $12.95**

Of Heaven and Earth: Essays Presented at the First Sitchin Studies Day, edited by Zecharia Sitchin. ISBN 1-885395-17-5 • 164 pages • 5 1/2 x 8 1/2 • trade paper • illustrated • $14.95

God Games: What Do You Do Forever?, by Neil Freer. ISBN 1-885395-39-6 • 312 pages • 6 x 9 • trade paper • $19.95

Past Shock: The Origin of Religion and Its Impact on the Human Soul, by Jack Barranger. ISBN 1-885395-08-6 • 126 pages • 6 x 9 • trade paper • illustrated • $12.95

Triumph of the Human Spirit: The Greatest Achievements of the Human Soul and How Its Power Can Change Your Life, by Paul Tice. ISBN 1-885395-57-4 • 295 pages • 6 x 9 • trade paper • illustrated • $19.95

Space Travelers and the Genesis of the Human Form: Evidence of Intelligent Contact in the Solar System, by Joan d'Arc. ISBN 1-58509-127-8 • 208 pages • 6 x 9 • trade paper • illustrated • $18.95

Mysteries Explored: The Search for Human Origins, UFOs, and Religious Beginnings, by Jack Barranger and Paul Tice. ISBN 1-58509-101-4 • 104 pages • 6 x 9 • trade paper • $12.95

Mushrooms and Mankind: The Impact of Mushrooms on Human Consciousness and Religion, by James Arthur. ISBN 1-58509-151-0 • 103 pages • 6 x 9 • trade paper • $12.95

Vril or Vital Magnetism, with an Introduction by Paul Tice. ISBN 1-58509-030-1 • 124 pages • 5 1/2 x 8 1/2 • trade paper • $12.95

The Odic Force: Letters on Od and Magnetism, by Karl von Reichenbach. ISBN 1-58509-001-8 • 192 pages • 6 x 9 • trade paper • $15.95

The New Revelation: The Coming of a New Spiritual Paradigm, by Arthur Conan Doyle. ISBN 1-58509-220-7 • 124 pages • 6 x 9 • trade paper • $12.95

The Astral World: Its Scenes, Dwellers, and Phenomena, by Swami Panchadasi. ISBN 1-58509-071-9 • 104 pages • 6 x 9 • trade paper • $11.95

Reason and Belief: The Impact of Scientific Discovery on Religious and Spiritual Faith, by Sir Oliver Lodge. ISBN 1-58509-226-6 • 180 pages • 6 x 9 • trade paper • $17.95

William Blake: A Biography, by Basil De Selincourt. ISBN 1-58509-225-8 • 384 pages • 6 x 9 • trade paper • $28.95

The Divine Pymander: And Other Writings of Hermes Trismegistus, translated by John D. Chambers. ISBN 1-58509-046-8 • 196 pages • 6 x 9 • trade paper • $16.95

Theosophy and The Secret Doctrine, by Harriet L. Henderson. Includes *H.P. Blavatsky: An Outline of Her Life,* by Herbert Whyte. ISBN 1-58509-075-1 • 132 pages • 6 x 9 • trade paper • $13.95

The Light of Egypt, Volume One: The Science of the Soul and the Stars, by Thomas H. Burgoyne. ISBN 1-58509-051-4 • 320 pages • 6 x 9 • trade paper • illustrated • $24.95

The Light of Egypt, Volume Two: The Science of the Soul and the Stars, by Thomas H. Burgoyne. ISBN 1-58509-052-2 • 224 pages • 6 x 9 • trade paper • illustrated • $17.95

The Jumping Frog and 18 Other Stories: 19 Unforgettable Mark Twain Stories, by Mark Twain. ISBN 1-58509-200-2 • 128 pages • 6 x 9 • trade paper • $12.95

The Devil's Dictionary: A Guidebook for Cynics, by Ambrose Bierce. ISBN 1-58509-016-6 • 144 pages • 6 x 9 • trade paper • $12.95

The Smoky God: Or The Voyage to the Inner World, by Willis George Emerson. ISBN 1-58509-067-0 • 184 pages • 6 x 9 • trade paper • illustrated • $15.95

A Short History of the World, by H.G. Wells. ISBN 1-58509-211-8 • 320 pages • 6 x 9 • trade paper • $24.95

The Voyages and Discoveries of the Companions of Columbus, by Washington Irving. ISBN 1-58509-500-1 • 352 pages • 6 x 9 • hard cover • $39.95

History of Baalbek, by Michel Alouf. ISBN 1-58509-063-8 • 196 pages • 5 x 8 • trade paper • illustrated • $15.95

Ancient Egyptian Masonry: The Building Craft, by Sommers Clarke and R. Engelback. ISBN 1-58509-059-X • 350 pages • 6 x 9 • trade paper • illustrated • $26.95

That Old Time Religion: The Story of Religious Foundations, by Jordan Maxwell and Paul Tice. ISBN 1-58509-100-6 • 103 pages • 6 x 9 • trade paper • $12.95

The Book of Enoch: A Work of Visionary Revelation and Prophecy, Revealing Divine Secrets and Fantastic Information about Creation, Salvation, Heaven and Hell, translated by R. H. Charles. ISBN 1-58509-019-0 • 152 pages • 5 1/2 x 8 1/2 • trade paper • $13.95

The Book of Enoch: Translated from the Editor's Ethiopic Text and Edited with an Enlarged Introduction, Notes and Indexes, Together with a Reprint of the Greek Fragments, edited by R. H. Charles. ISBN 1-58509-080-8 • 448 pages • 6 x 9 • trade paper • $34.95

The Book of the Secrets of Enoch, translated from the Slavonic by W. R. Morfill. Edited, with Introduction and Notes by R. H. Charles. ISBN 1-58509-020-4 • 148 pages • 5 1/2 x 8 1/2 • trade paper • $13.95

Enuma Elish: The Seven Tablets of Creation, Volume One, by L. W. King. ISBN 1-58509-041-7 • 236 pages • 6 x 9 • trade paper • illustrated • $18.95

Enuma Elish: The Seven Tablets of Creation, Volume Two, by L. W. King. ISBN 1-58509-042-5 • 260 pages • 6 x 9 • trade paper • illustrated • $19.95

Enuma Elish, Volumes One and Two: The Seven Tablets of Creation, by L. W. King. Two volumes from above bound as one. ISBN 1-58509-043-3 • 496 pages • 6 x 9 • trade paper • illustrated • $38.90

The Archko Volume: Documents that Claim Proof to the Life, Death, and Resurrection of Christ, by Drs. McIntosh and Twyman. ISBN 1-58509-082-4 • 248 pages • 6 x 9 • trade paper • $20.95

The Lost Language of Symbolism: An Inquiry into the Origin of Certain Letters, Words, Names, Fairy-Tales, Folklore, and Mythologies, by Harold Bayley. ISBN 1-58509-070-0 • 384 pages • 6 x 9 • trade paper • $27.95

The Book of Jasher: A Suppressed Book that was Removed from the Bible, Referred to in Joshua and Second Samuel, translated by Albinus Alcuin (800 AD). ISBN 1-58509-081-6 • 304 pages • 6 x 9 • trade paper • $24.95

The Bible's Most Embarrassing Moments, with an Introduction by Paul Tice. ISBN 1-58509-025-5 • 172 pages • 5 x 8 • trade paper • $14.95

History of the Cross: The Pagan Origin and Idolatrous Adoption and Worship of the Image, by Henry Dana Ward. ISBN 1-58509-056-5 • 104 pages • 6 x 9 • trade paper • illustrated • $11.95

Was Jesus Influenced by Buddhism? A Comparative Study of the Lives and Thoughts of Gautama and Jesus, by Dwight Goddard. ISBN 1-58509-027-1 • 252 pages • 6 x 9 • trade paper • $19.95

History of the Christian Religion to the Year Two Hundred, by Charles B. Waite. ISBN 1-885395-15-9 • 556 pages • 6 x 9 • hard cover • $25.00

Symbols, Sex, and the Stars, by Ernest Busenbark. ISBN 1-885395-19-1 • 396 pages • 5 1/2 x 8 1/2 • trade paper • $22.95

History of the First Council of Nice: A World's Christian Convention, A.D. 325, by Dean Dudley. ISBN 1-58509-023-9 • 132 pages • 5 1/2 x 8 1/2 • trade paper • $12.95

The World's Sixteen Crucified Saviors, by Kersey Graves. ISBN 1-58509-018-2 • 436 pages • 5 1/2 x 8 1/2 • trade paper • $29.95

Babylonian Influence on the Bible and Popular Beliefs: A Comparative Study of Genesis I.2, by A. Smythe Palmer. ISBN 1-58509-000-X • 124 pages • 6 x 9 • trade paper • $12.95

Biography of Satan: Exposing the Origins of the Devil, by Kersey Graves. ISBN 1-885395-11-6 • 168 pages • 5 1/2 x 8 1/2 • trade paper • $13.95

The Malleus Maleficarum: The Notorious Handbook Once Used to Condemn and Punish "Witches", by Heinrich Kramer and James Sprenger. ISBN 1-58509-098-0 • 332 pages • 6 x 9 • trade paper • $25.95

Crux Ansata: An Indictment of the Roman Catholic Church, by H. G. Wells. ISBN 1-58509-210-X • 160 pages • 6 x 9 • trade paper • $14.95

Emanuel Swedenborg: The Spiritual Columbus, by U.S.E. (William Spear). ISBN 1-58509-096-4 • 208 pages • 6 x 9 • trade paper • $17.95

Dragons and Dragon Lore, by Ernest Ingersoll. ISBN 1-58509-021-2 • 228 pages • 6 x 9 • trade paper • illustrated • $17.95

The Vision of God, by Nicholas of Cusa. ISBN 1-58509-004-2 • 160 pages • 5 x 8 • trade paper • $13.95

The Historical Jesus and the Mythical Christ: Separating Fact From Fiction, by Gerald Massey. ISBN 1-58509-073-5 • 244 pages • 6 x 9 • trade paper • $18.95

Gog and Magog: The Giants in Guildhall; Their Real and Legendary History, with an Account of Other Giants at Home and Abroad, by F.W. Fairholt. ISBN 1-58509-084-0 • 172 pages • 6 x 9 • trade paper • $16.95

The Origin and Evolution of Religion, by Albert Churchward. ISBN 1-58509-078-6 • 504 pages • 6 x 9 • trade paper • $39.95

The Origin of Biblical Traditions, by Albert T. Clay. ISBN 1-58509-065-4 • 220 pages • 5 1/2 x 8 1/2 • trade paper • $17.95

Aryan Sun Myths, by Sarah Elizabeth Titcomb, Introduction by Charles Morris. ISBN 1-58509-069-7 • 192 pages • 6 x 9 • trade paper • $15.95

The Social Record of Christianity, by Joseph McCabe. Includes **The Lies and Fallacies of the Encyclopedia Britannica,** ISBN 1-58509-215-0 • 204 pages • 6 x 9 • trade paper • $17.95

The History of the Christian Religion and Church During the First Three Centuries, by Dr. Augustus Neander. ISBN 1-58509-077-8 • 112 pages • 6 x 9 • trade paper • $12.95

Ancient Symbol Worship: Influence of the Phallic Idea in the Religions of Antiquity, by Hodder M. Westropp and C. Staniland Wake. ISBN 1-58509-048-4 • 120 pages • 6 x 9 • trade paper • illustrated • $12.95

The Gnosis: Or Ancient Wisdom in the Christian Scriptures, by William Kingsland. ISBN 1-58509-047-6 • 232 pages • 6 x 9 • trade paper • $18.95

The Evolution of the Idea of God: An Inquiry into the Origin of Religions, by Grant Allen. ISBN 1-58509-074-3 • 160 pages • 6 x 9 • trade paper • $14.95

Sun Lore of All Ages: A Survey of Solar Mythology, Folklore, Customs, Worship, Festivals, and Superstition, by William Tyler Olcott. ISBN 1-58509-044-1 • 316 pages • 6 x 9 • trade paper • $24.95

Nature Worship: An Account of Phallic Faiths and Practices Ancient and Modern, by the Author of Phallicism with an Introduction by Tedd St. Rain. ISBN 1-58509-049-2 • 112 pages • 6 x 9 • trade paper • illustrated • $12.95

Life and Religion, by Max Muller. ISBN 1-885395-10-8 • 237 pages • 5 1/2 x 8 1/2 • trade paper • $14.95

Jesus: God, Man, or Myth? An Examination of the Evidence, by Herbert Cutner. ISBN 1-58509-072-7 • 304 pages • 6 x 9 • trade paper • $23.95

Pagan and Christian Creeds: Their Origin and Meaning, by Edward Carpenter. ISBN 1-58509-024-7 • 316 pages • 5 1/2 x 8 1/2 • trade paper • $24.95

The Christ Myth: A Study, by Elizabeth Evans. ISBN 1-58509-037-9 • 136 pages • 6 x 9 • trade paper • $13.95

Popery: Foe of the Church and the Republic, by Joseph F. Van Dyke. ISBN 1-58509-058-1 • 336 pages • 6 x 9 • trade paper • illustrated • $25.95

Career of Religious Ideas, by Hudson Tuttle. ISBN 1-58509-066-2 • 172 pages • 5 x 8 • trade paper • $15.95

Buddhist Suttas: Major Scriptural Writings from Early Buddhism, by T.W. Rhys Davids. ISBN 1-58509-079-4 • 376 pages • 6 x 9 • trade paper • $27.95

Early Buddhism, by T. W. Rhys Davids. Includes **Buddhist Ethics: The Way to Salvation?,** by Paul Tice. ISBN 1-58509-076-X • 112 pages • 6 x 9 • trade paper • $12.95

The Fountain-Head of Religion: A Comparative Study of the Principal Religions of the World and a Manifestation of their Common Origin from the Vedas, by Ganga Prasad. ISBN 1-58509-054-9 • 276 pages • 6 x 9 • trade paper • $22.95

India: What Can It Teach Us?, by Max Muller. ISBN 1-58509-064-6 • 284 pages • 5 1/2 x 8 1/2 • trade paper • $22.95

Matrix of Power: How the World has Been Controlled by Powerful People Without Your Knowledge, by Jordan Maxwell. ISBN 1-58509-120-0 • 104 pages • 6 x 9 • trade paper • $12.95

Cyberculture Counterconspiracy: A Steamshovel Web Reader, Volume One, edited by Kenn Thomas. ISBN 1-58509-125-1 • 180 pages • 6 x 9 • trade paper • illustrated • $16.95

Cyberculture Counterconspiracy: A Steamshovel Web Reader, Volume Two, edited by Kenn Thomas. ISBN 1-58509-126-X • 132 pages • 6 x 9 • trade paper • illustrated • $13.95

Oklahoma City Bombing: The Suppressed Truth, by Jon Rappoport. ISBN 1-885395-22-1 • 112 pages • 5 1/2 x 8 1/2 • trade paper • $12.95

Secret Societies and Subversive Movements, by Nesta H. Webster. ISBN 1-58509-092-1 • 432 pages • 6 x 9 • trade paper • $29.95

The Secret Doctrine of the Rosicrucians, by Magus Incognito. ISBN 1-58509-091-3 • 256 pages • 6 x 9 • trade paper • $20.95

The Origin and Evolution of Freemasonry: Connected with the Origin and Evolution of the Human Race, by Albert Churchward. ISBN 1-58509-029-8 • 240 pages • 6 x 9 • trade paper • $18.95

The Lost Key: An Explanation and Application of Masonic Symbols, by Prentiss Tucker. ISBN 1-58509-050-6 • 192 pages • 6 x 9 • trade paper • illustrated • $15.95

The Character, Claims, and Practical Workings of Freemasonry, by Rev. C.G. Finney. ISBN 1-58509-094-8 • 288 pages • 6 x 9 • trade paper • $22.95

The Secret World Government or "The Hidden Hand": The Unrevealed in History, by Maj.-Gen., Count Cherep-Spiridovich. ISBN 1-58509-093-X • 203 pages • 6 x 9 • trade paper • $17.95

The Magus, Book One: A Complete System of Occult Philosophy, by Francis Barrett. ISBN 1-58509-031-X • 200 pages • 6 x 9 • trade paper • illustrated • $16.95

The Magus, Book Two: A Complete System of Occult Philosophy, by Francis Barrett. ISBN 1-58509-032-8 • 220 pages • 6 x 9 • trade paper • illustrated • $17.95

The Magus, Book One and Two: A Complete System of Occult Philosophy, by Francis Barrett. ISBN 1-58509-033-6 • 420 pages • 6 x 9 • trade paper • illustrated • $34.90

The Key of Solomon The King, by S. Liddell MacGregor Mathers. ISBN 1-58509-022-0 • 152 pages • 6 x 9 • trade paper • illustrated • $12.95

Magic and Mystery in Tibet, by Alexandra David-Neel. ISBN 1-58509-097-2 • 352 pages • 6 x 9 • trade paper • $26.95

The Comte de St. Germain, by I. Cooper Oakley. ISBN 1-58509-068-9 • 280 pages • 6 x 9 • trade paper • illustrated • $22.95

Alchemy Rediscovered and Restored, by A. Cockren. ISBN 1-58509-028-X • 156 pages • 5 1/2 x 8 1/2 • trade paper • $13.95

The 6th and 7th Books of Moses, with an Introduction by Paul Tice. ISBN 1-58509-045-X • 188 pages • 6 x 9 • trade paper • illustrated • $16.95

CPSIA information can be obtained
at www.ICGtesting.com
Printed in the USA
BVHW070103040920
587909BV00002B/135

9 781585 095605